YOUR GARDEN SOIL

YOUR GARDEN SOIL

HARRY MADDOX

With illustrations by Molly Maddox

DAVID & CHARLES
NEWTON ABBOT   LONDON
NORTH POMFRET (VT)   VANCOUVER

ISBN 0 7153 6661 0

Set in 11 on 13pt Garamond and printed in
Great Britain by Latimer Trend & Company Ltd Plymouth
for David & Charles (Holdings) Limited
South Devon House Newton Abbot Devon

Published in the United States of America by
David & Charles Inc
North Pomfret Vermont 05053 USA

Published in Canada by
Douglas David & Charles Limited
3645 McKechnie Drive West Vancouver BC

CONTENTS

LIST OF ILLUSTRATIONS

PLATES

7

IN TEXT

PREFACE

This book attempts to popularise some of the findings of the sciences of soils and plant nutrition. It owes its origin to the work of the late Firman E. Bear. After many years of amateur gardening in different countries, I happened to read Bear's *Soils in Relation to Crop Growth*, and felt much like Keats on first looking into Chapman's Homer – that a whole new territory lay before me, of which until then I had been only dimly aware; and that the patient work of generations of soil scientists, so ably summarised there, ought to be more widely known to gardeners. Bear was an eminent chemist, who wrote for agriculturalists, but clearly the basic principles of plant growth applied equally to the garden.

Yet few gardeners are aware of the great mass of scientific knowledge about the soil that has accumulated in the last century. There are understandable reasons for this. Practical men often distrust book-learning; and in the past much traditional gardening lore was passed on orally from one generation to the next. Much of the traditional lore is essentially sound. And indeed there is no substitute for the countless observations, the trial and error and the detailed care of the individual gardener. But the mere practice of gardening, however adequate for a particular plot, will not satisfy intellectual curiosity; and sometimes seems to resemble a series of superstitions or magic rituals, which are performed mainly for the benefit of commercial interests. Moreover, mere practical lore may involve misconceptions which stand in the way of the acquisition of further knowledge.

There are of course formidable obstacles in the way of reaching any basic understanding of soils and plants. Often it is necessary to descend below the ordinary perceptual world to the complicated microworld of cells, molecules and atoms. And then each of the interrelated disciplines of soils, chemistry, botany and plant physiology appears to demand years of specialist study. Finally, knowledge is incomplete, sometimes conflicting.

In writing this book I have emphasised those topics which seemed of practical relevance. I have tried to write as simply as the subject-matter allows, but have not tried to avoid the use of scientific concepts in those contexts in which their omission would lead to a loss of precision. The result is partly an explanatory account of soils, manures, lime, fertilisers and trace elements, and also a reference book which gives practical recommendations. Most chapters can be read or consulted as units, and I have not sought to avoid the repetition of important points which need to be made in several contexts.

Dr C. Bould, Head of Plant Nutrition at the Long Ashton Research Station, was kind enough to scrutinise the manuscript from the point of view of scientific accuracy, and made a great many valuable suggestions. Such faults as remain are of course mine alone.

To Mrs Prue Hutton I owe thanks for her faultless typing of the manuscript.

H.M.

CHAPTER I

PLANT GROWTH

So from the root
Springs lighter the green stalk, from thence the leaves
More aery, last the bright consummate flow'r
Spirits odorous breathes

(Milton)

The food of plants comes from soil, water and air. Plant tissue consists mostly of carbohydrate, that is of carbon, hydrogen and oxygen. Plants get these three elements from air and water. Water is absorbed by the roots. Carbon is absorbed from the carbon dioxide of the air, through the minute pores in the leaf surface called stomata. The energy of sunlight falling on the leaf is used to split the water molecules in the leaf into hydrogen and oxygen. The oxygen fraction of the water is released through the stomata. The hydrogen fraction is used to reduce carbon from its low-energy state in carbon dioxide to a higher level of energy in the form of glucose $C_6H_{12}O_6$.

The glucose in turn is exported from the leaf: some is converted into more complex substances and moves to the growing points; some is stored in the stem or root. In order to evolve these more complex substances, such as proteins and fats, mineral nutrients such as nitrogen, phosphorus and sulphur have to be combined with the carbohydrate manufactured in the leaf. These and other minerals are taken up by the roots from the soil solution, and carried upwards in the plant in the transpiration stream.

Water and mineral solutes are taken up mainly by the root tips and by the fine root hairs which lie near the root tips.

From these the water rises in a continuous column of ducts and vessels, the xylem (wood), through the stem and through the leaf veins, finally evaporating in the air spaces of the leaf. Evaporation in the leaf produces a pressure deficit which enables the water

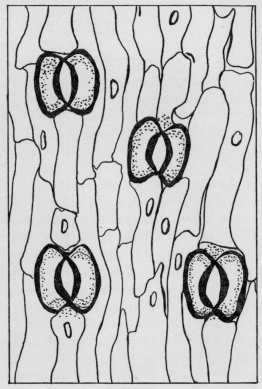

Stomata in the leaf of the Crown Imperial

to rise against the force of gravity. About 99 per cent of the water absorbed is transpired.

Another system of ducts and vessels which, together with the xylem, makes up the vascular system of the plant, runs more or less parallel with the xylem. This is the phloem, a system of long tubes through which the sugars pass into the stem and move upwards to new growth or downwards to the root. Phloem and xylem are not entirely separate, however, so that mineral nutrients being carried up with the water in the xylem can move across to the phloem. And some minerals carried to the leaf in the xylem

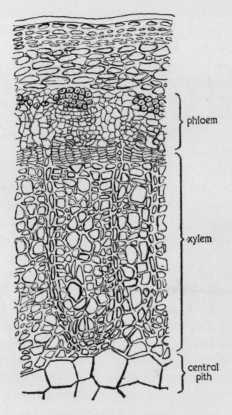

Cross section of a segment of the stem of a
tulip poplar, a typical woody didcot

can be re-exported in the phloem from the leaf to all parts of the plant. Likewise some of the mineral compounds in the phloem can move laterally, enter the transpiration stream in the xylem, and be carried rapidly upwards. In this way most minerals and mineral compounds can circulate to all parts of the plant.

Trnaspiration in any growing plant can readily be demonstrated by covering the plant with a glass jar or polythene bag, and noting the rapid accumulation of moisture on the inside.

ROOTS

Many plants send down their roots far deeper into the soil than appearances suggest. In well-drained porous soils, roots often penetrate to a depth of 4–5ft. A deep-rooting habit enables plants to obtain water and nutrients from the deeper soil layers, and so to withstand periods of drought. A deep soil is essential for fruit-trees especially, some 2ft or 3ft of well-drained soil being considered the minimum depth for orchard sites. Such deep soils are most often to be found at the bottom of slopes, in the alluvium of valleys, and in soils derived from glacial drift.

Heavy clay soils, whatever their depth, are difficult for roots to penetrate. Roots have to grow through the soil by tracing intricate and winding paths through small channels and cracks. A young plant which is actively growing may produce some miles of new roots each day in an open well-aerated soil. But a compact clay not only offers physical resistance to the passage of roots, but contains so little oxygen that roots cannot respire. Clover roots, for example, which extend to almost 4ft in an open porous soil, are confined to the top 10in in a clay soil

If roots find ample supplies of moisture and nutrients in the topsoil, they branch freely near the surface. But sands and loams dry out rapidly in their surface layers. Root systems in these lighter soils therefore go deeper in order to reach supplies of water in the subsoil, and since these soils are open, the roots can branch freely. Hence plants grown in these soils have deeper and more extensive root systems than those grown on clay.

It is true that the feeding roots of most plants are most widespread in the topsoil; for the topsoil is usually better aerated and more fertile than the subsoil But under favourable conditions roots also extend downwards and tap water in the deeper layers. In fact they proliferate at whatever depths a good supply of water and nutrients can be found.

There are of course species differences in rooting habits. Some plants such as brassicas or lettuces are shallow-rooting; others such as tomatoes or parsnips are deep-rooting. Some trees such as beech or sycamore fill the topsoil with a mass of fibrous roots; others such as the ash have deeper and more extensive roots. But for any given species the depth of root penetration depends on

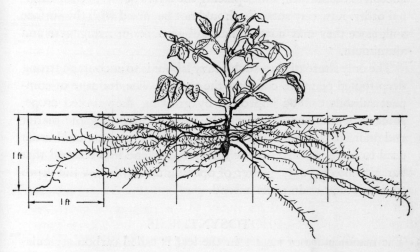

Root system of a potato – a shallow-rooting plant – at 36 days

soil conditions – on texture, moisture, aeration, and on the depth and fertility of the soil.

Roots will normally grow only into a moist soil. But they also need air, and if the soil is waterlogged and does not contain enough oxygen, they quickly die. The root tips and root hairs near the tips are especially sensitive to lack of air. This is often evident in pot plants which have been so over-watered that the soil contains no air. Hence the need for drainage crocks in the bottom of pots, and of grit and coarse sand in potting mixtures. In the same way the roots of trees and plants may be killed in waterlogged soil. Increasing wetness of the soil results in a declining rate of root growth in all plants except those, such as willows,

B

which are adapted to wet soils and can transfer oxygen to their roots from their aerial parts.

If a subsoil contains a hardpan or is a poorly drained fine clay, it needs to be broken up both to admit air and to permit the easier passage of roots. In the garden this entails the laborious work of trenching and double-trenching, taking care not to bring the subsoil to the surface, and replacing the layers of soil in their original order. Raw clay subsoils should not be mixed with the surface soil, since they may contain harmful amounts of manganese and aluminium.

The only alternative to such heavy labour is to encourage strong deep-rooted plants to cultivate the ground. The drainage of compact subsoils can be improved by growing deep-rooted crops, some of whose roots, when they die, will leave organic matter and drainage channels deep in the soil. Chicory, lupins and burnet used to be recommended for this purpose, and it is claimed that parsnips also have the power of opening up clay below the depth to which their main roots extend.

PHOTOSYNTHESIS

The manufacture of sugars in the leaf is called carbon assimilation or photosynthesis – the making or synthesising of food with the aid of light. All life depends on this process; and the food of all animals is derived from green plants. It is of more than theoretical interest, since photosynthesis may be controlled by controlling the supply of light, water and carbon dioxide. Photosynthesis takes place only in the leaf and in the green parts of the plant which contain chlorophyll, the mixture of pigments which gives them their green colour. The chlorophyll is contained in special bodies called chloroplasts. A typical leaf consists of a layer of palisade cells which contain many chloroplasts, and a spongy lower layer of cells, also containing chloroplasts.

Carbon dioxide enters the leaf through the stomata and diffuses into the air spaces inside the leaf. There it is dissolved in water, since the cell walls surrounding the air spaces are wet with water that has come up from the roots.

The rate of photosynthesis depends on:

1 light intensity;
2 temperature;
3 supply of water;
4 supply of carbon dioxide;
5 the chlorophyll content of the chloroplast cells.

Any of these five factors, if deficient, will limit the rate of photosynthesis, and hence the rate of growth.

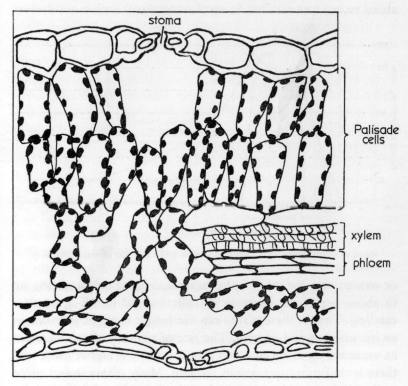

Transverse section of a rhubarb leaf. Chloroplasts shown in black

LIGHT INTENSITY AND DURATION

Different plant species have different rates of photosynthesis. A pumpkin can use a much greater light intensity than a brussels sprout. Some plants, including many broad-leaved evergreens, prefer shade. They can carry on photosynthesis at lower light intensities than those which grow in the sun. Plants should therefore be positioned in relation to light and shade in terms of what is known of their light requirements. And gardeners need to observe for how long the various sections of their gardens are in sun and in shade at different seasons. In shade plants, such as woodland flowers and ferns, the rate of photosynthesis increases with light intensity up to about 0·1 of the intensity of full sunlight, which is about 10,000 foot candles. In sun-loving plants such as sunflowers

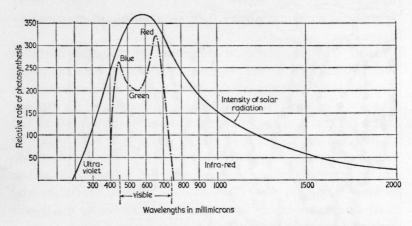

Rates of photosynthesis in different wavelengths of light of equal intensity

or nasturtiums the rate of photosynthesis goes on increasing up to about 0·7 of the intensity of full sunlight (6,000–7,000 foot candles). That is, these plants can use bright sunlight to maintain an increased rate of growth. The rate of photosynthesis increases in tomatoes up to about 4,500 foot candles. At higher intensities there is no further increase in the rate. Many plants in fact grow well at light intensities lower than the intensity of full sunlight. Most grow well when they are in sun for about half the daylight hours.

Of all the essentials for plant growth, light was one of the last to be successfully controlled. The supply of artificial light to

supplement or replace daylight has proved to be a complex subject. Although green plants are affected by the whole of the visible
spectrum in much the same way as the human eye, the peak response of the chloroplasts is to red light, with a lesser peak in the
blue region. The green/yellow wavelengths to which the human
eye is most sensitive are relatively ineffective in photosynthesis
but, naturally, all the spectral emission which is present in sunlight
is important to normal growth.

No lamp has a spectral emission which resembles that of daylight. Ordinary incandescent household lamps emit mostly red
light, but also a good deal of infra-red radiation. The best current
approximation to the plant's light requirements is provided by
fluorescent tubes of white or warm-white colour.

Apart from the technical difficulties of providing light of
sufficient intensity at the required wavelengths, different plants
respond in different ways to the duration of artificial illumination.
The so-called short-day plants which are natives of the tropics,
where the day is never longer than twelve to thirteen hours, fail
to flower if day length is artificially prolonged. Such plants as
cosmos, chrysanthemums and dahlias, being short-day plants, do
not flower in temperate regions until the shorter days of late
summer. Long-day plants, which include many vegetables and
most summer-blooming flowers, mature more rapidly and flower
earlier when artificially illuminated.

The light integral is a measure of both the intensity and the
duration of light. In northern latitudes the daily midwinter light
integral is only about one-tenth of the midsummer level. This is
partly because winter daylight in Northern Europe is only about
eight hours against the summer daylight of about sixteen hours,
and partly because light intensity in winter, when the sun is lower
and its rays have to pass through a thicker air mass, is much less
than in summer. Hence in northern latitudes there is little growth
in winter without artificial light.

High light intensity is even more necessary for the formation
of fruit and seeds than it is for vegetative growth. The best and
largest apples, for example, grow on the high branches where they

Cosmos, a short-day plant which is a
native of Mexico

get full sun, while the fruits growing on the lower and more
shaded inside branches are smaller. Bright light also favours flowering as witness the abundance of flowers in the intense light of
high altitudes. By contrast, in the shade of woods there are few
summer flowers.

TEMPERATURE

A temperature of about 20° C results in maximum photosynthesis
for the plants of temperate climates. The graph shows the rate of
photosynthesis of potato leaves as temperature varies.

It is a common observation that plants grow fastest when the weather becomes warm. Between 0° C and 20° C the rate of photosynthesis rises regularly with rise in temperature. For every 10° C increase in temperature over this range, the rate of photosynthesis is about doubled. There are a few plants such as conifers and winter wheat which can grow at temperatures below freezing-point, but in most plants growth ceases at temperatures around

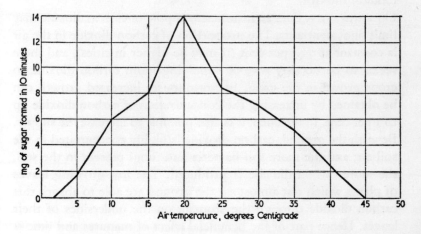

Effect of temperature on photosynthesis in potato leaves

0° C. Normally light and temperature co-vary, and it is therefore not easy to separate their effect. But it is found that at low light intensities temperature increases have little effect on photosynthesis. Increasing a greenhouse temperature to 20° C, for example, would result in little growth on a dull overcast day.

WATER

Most of the water which plants take up is lost by transpiration from the leaves. As temperature rises, the rate of transpiration increases until the plants wilt. When wilting-point is reached the leaf stomata close, thus partly preventing further losses of moisture. When the stomata close, carbon dioxide cannot enter the plant and photosynthesis ceases. Plants with shallow roots, and those that prefer shade, suffer more in the heat and wilt at a lower temperature than sun-loving plants. There are great differences among species. Petunias, for example, do not wilt in hot dry conditions; whereas plants such as hydrangeas, which have a high transpiration rate, soon exhaust the available supplies of water on a hot day.

CARBON DIOXIDE

On warm sunny days an insufficient supply of carbon dioxide may limit photosynthesis. The proportion of carbon dioxide in the air is constant at 0·03 per cent (it may be higher in cities), and there seems to be no easy way of supplying more carbon dioxide to crops grown in the open. In greenhouses increased growth can be obtained by increasing the concentration of carbon dioxide up to 1 per cent. In the open, it is also possible to increase the supply. Beneath the ground, carbon dioxide is highly concentrated in the soil air; and the more soil bacteria and fungi present in the soil, the more carbon dioxide is produced. The low-growing leaves of plants which rest almost on the ground are able to absorb this carbon dioxide through the stomata on the undersides of their leaves. Hence part of the beneficial effect of manures and lime is that, by increasing the numbers of soil inhabitants, they increase the supply of carbon dioxide.

CHLOROPHYLL

Photosynthesis is not normally limited by deficiencies of chlorophyll. But magnesium and nitrogen must be absorbed from the soil in order to form chlorophyll. Iron, sulphur and manganese are also needed. Deficiencies of these elements in the plant may therefore reduce the amounts of chlorophyll which can be made, and hence decrease the rate of growth. Photosynthesis can thus be directly affected by an infertile soil.

The factors which influence photosynthesis are interrelated. Light intensity and temperature usually go together. The absorption of water increases with temperature. An increase of light intensity also increases the uptake of nutrients from the soil.

Given a hot sunny day, shortages of water and of carbon dioxide are most likely to limit the rate of photosynthesis.

RESPIRATION

If pea seeds are placed in a glass of water, they will swell up and start to germinate. But after a few days they will become mouldy and die. Now, if the seeds are placed on damp blotting paper in a covered glass dish, they will germinate and grow normally. In this latter case the seeds are in contact with air and can obtain oxygen for respiration. In the first case the seeds die for lack of oxygen.

Respiration is the process by which the carbohydrate which has been made in photosynthesis, or which has been stored in the seed, is converted into energy for work. Just as men and animals need energy for their bodily activities, plants need energy to take up nutrients, to grow, and to push their roots down into the soil. Photosynthesis converts light energy into the chemical energy of sugar. Respiration makes this chemical energy available for work. Photosynthesis goes on only in the day. Respiration goes on day and night. In the day the plant will usually be making four or five times as much food as is being used up in respiration. So the end-products of photosynthesis – oxygen and water – are released into the air. But at night, when photosynthesis stops, the end-products of respiration – carbon dioxide and water – diffuse out of plants. In other words, when photosynthesis is not going on, oxygen is absorbed and carbon dioxide is given off, as in the respiration of animals and men. All living cells respire. Even the stored potato needs oxygen for respiration.

The aerial parts of plants can obtain oxygen from the air. But roots have to get their oxygen from the air in the soil. If the air of the atmosphere cannot diffuse down into the upper layers of the soil, the growing tips of roots will be starved of oxygen.

Photosynthesis and respiration are opposite processes: in photosynthesis energy is stored, in respiration it is released. When carbohydrate needs to be stored in the plant, as in the fruiting of apples or tomatoes, photosynthesis needs to be much greater than respiration. The rate of respiration depends largely on temperature. So cool nights in which respiration is low, following sunny days in which photosynthesis is high, result in good-quality fruit. In the greenhouse, similarly, cool night conditions favour the flowering of such plants as carnations. Potatoes need cool nights so that the starches made in the day can be stored in the root tubers at night; if night temperatures are high, few tubers are formed.

LIMITING FACTORS

Altogether then, light, heat, water, oxygen, carbon dioxide and mineral nutrients are all essential for growth. There is a certain minimum requirement for each of these six factors, and if any one of them is not present in this minimum amount, an increased supply of any of the other five will be of no advantage. For each factor there can be said to be crude minima, optima and maxima, although the factors interact and optimal values vary with the duration of exposure and the stage of plant development. The approximate values of these levels are:

	Minimum	Optimum	Maximum
Light	2 foot candles	1,500 foot candles	12,000 foot candles
Temperature of soil and air	0° C	25° C	50° C
Water in soil	Wilting-point	Field capacity	Above field capacity (waterlogged)
Oxygen (in soil air)	2 % of soil air	15–21 %	—
Carbon dioxide (in atmosphere)	0·0005 % of atmospheric air	0·03–0·3 %	Continuous exposure to more than 0·3 %
Minerals, eg nitrogen in soil	5ppm (parts per million in soil solution)	150ppm	350ppm

These are merely illustrative values. Sun plants can use more light than shade plants. Siberian conifers can grow in subzero temperatures. The prickly pear survives in the dry soil of the desert. Moreover, the optima not only vary among plant species but depend on the levels of the other factors. Nevertheless, for each species there can be said to be a minimum value of each of the six factors below which growth cannot take place. Likewise, at the other extreme, each factor may be present in such excess that normal growth is prevented and death may ensue.

If any of the six factors is present in such small amounts that plant growth is much restricted it is said to be a *limiting* factor, and no improvement can be effected until the deficiency is made good. And even when no factor is below the minimum level, the greatest improvements will result from making good those factors which lie furthest from the optima.

These manifold requirements of the plant need to be kept in mind since the object of gardening is often to grow plants far from their original climate and habitat, under conditions in which the optimum levels of the six factors are unlikely to be met.

LAW OF THE MINIMUM

Many attempts have been made to express precisely the relationship between the supply of mineral elements and the growth of plants. The law of the minimum, formulated by Liebig in 1840, stated that plant growth is limited by the element in shortest supply. Growth depends, of course, not only on the mineral nutrients but on light, temperature and moisture and indeed on a host of other factors. The main factors that limit growth in Northern Europe, for example, are light and temperature; in Australia, moisture, phosphorus and trace elements. The idea of a limiting factor follows readily from the idea that each of the essential elements is truly essential, in that no other element can be substituted for it. For each element has specific roles in plant physiology.

To illustrate this idea a common analogy is the behaviour of water in a barrel, of which the constituent timbers are of unequal height:

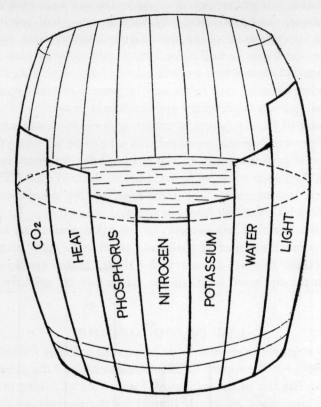

The barrel analogy. Yield, represented by the height of water in the barrel, is limited by the essential element in shortest supply – in this case nitrogen

If the height of water in the barrel is taken to represent yield or growth and the height of the individual timbers the amount of each element, yield must be limited by the element in shortest supply. Like all analogies the barrel analogy is over-simplified. Although an absolute deficiency of an element may prevent all growth, some improvement will occur when any of a number of less severe deficiencies are set right.

In the diagram it is assumed that a soil lacks nitrogen (N), phosphorus (P) and potassium (K), being very deficient in nitrogen, moderately deficient in phosphorus and little deficient in potassium. According to the law of the minimum, only an increase in the factor in shortest supply, nitrogen, will cause an

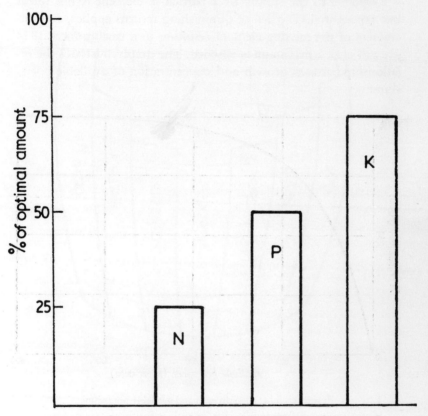

Interpretations of the law of the minimum

increase in growth. But according to the German plant physiolo gist Mitscherlich (1909), an increase in any of the three elements will increase growth. Unit increase of nitrogen will have the greatest effect, unit increase of phosphorus a somewhat lesser effect and unit increase of potassium the least effect.

Mitscherlich's law is closer to the facts than the law of the minimum, except in the case of nitrogen. Nitrogen is required in larger quantities than any other mineral, so that if nitrogen is grossly deficient, very little improvement in growth can be expected until an adequate supply of nitrogen is provided.

Response to the supply of a particular element is not linear but exponential. The law of diminishing returns applies, each increment of the missing element resulting in a smaller increase in growth until a maximum is reached. The graph illustrates the relationship between growth and concentration of available potassium:

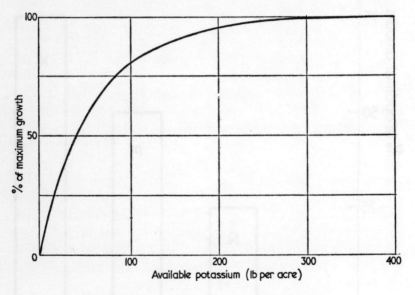

Relationship between growth and available potassium

Thus, if a particular element is very deficient, a small fertiliser dressing will produce a large and dramatic response, but further dressings have less and less effect until the point is reached at which further fertiliser has no effect, or even a negative effect.

From this discussion of limiting factors it follows first that it is usually futile to increase the supply of any one element whether, heat, light, water or mineral nutrient, without proportionately increasing the other limiting essentials; and secondly that large growth increments will often result from moderate applications of those elements which are lacking.

CHAPTER 2

SOIL FORMATION AND TEXTURE

A great while ago the world begun
with heigh ho the wind and the rain.
(Shakespeare)

The most striking feature of a soil map of the world is the great diversity of soils. Hundreds of different minerals are distributed over the earth's surface in varying amounts. The original rocks of the earth's crust, as it solidified from its molten state over the long ages of geological time, have everywhere been broken down and weathered by the elements. Many parts of the world have been several times submerged by seas and lakes, and layers of sedimentary rocks such as limestones and sandstones have formed over the original igneous rocks. The successive strata laid down by sedimentation have then been thrown up in the great earth movements which produced the Alps and the Himalayas. And more recently, in several Ice Ages, glaciers covered much of the earth, cutting through mountains, grinding rocks to fine particles and, as they melted, leaving behind a glacial drift of clay, sand and gravel, resulting in great local diversity of soils.

It is usually of more practical interest to know the history of a soil over the last ten years than over the aeons of time. Nevertheless, the general processes of soil formation, although mainly of interest to the soil geographer and pedologist, are still at work in the present.

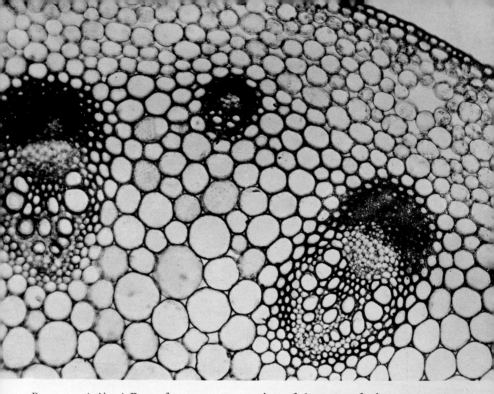

Page 33 (*Above*) Part of a transverse section of the stem of a buttercup, as seen through a microscope, showing vascular bundles; (*below*) effect of soil acidity on barley plants

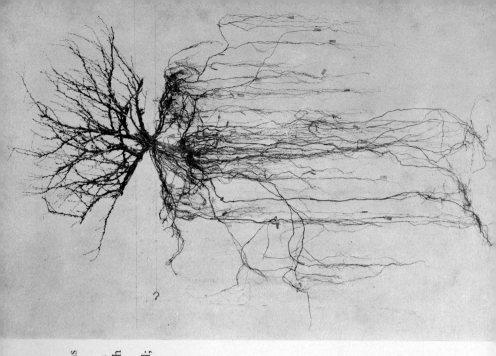

Page 34 Root systems of 8-year-old gooseberry plants grown in two parts of a field with sandy soil.
(*Left*) Unmanured soil; (*right*) received heavy dressing of farmyard manure in year of planting

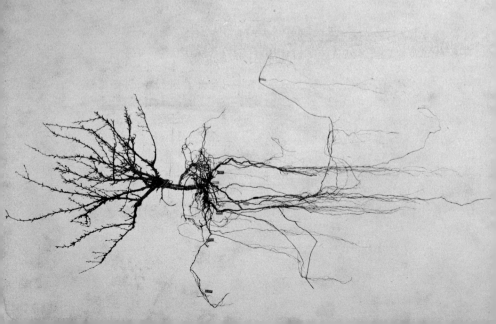

SOIL PROFILES

The study of soils is concerned not only with the top 6in or 10in which man cultivates, but with the deeper layers of soil, down to the parent rock, into which plant roots may extend. A vertical section through the soil is known as a profile. In the soil profile distinct layers or horizons can usually be distinguished. In scientific agriculture it is customary to dig pits several feet deep in order to examine the profile. Some idea of local profiles can be gained from ditches, trenches and other excavations. Gardeners need to dig down to a depth of 3ft or so, to see what lies beneath the surface soil.

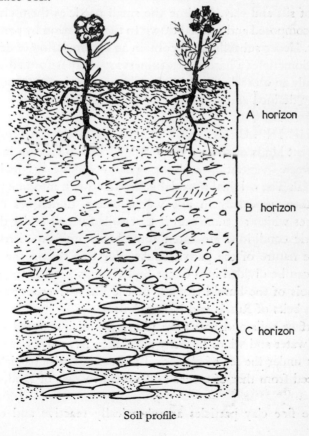

Soil profile

The layers or horizons in the profile are commonly referred to, in descending order, as the A, B and C horizons. In humid climates the top layer or A horizon is darker than the lower layers because it contains more humus and plant remains. Beneath the A horizon, the B horizon or subsoil is usually lighter in colour and often contains more clay. Beneath the B horizon lies the parent material, the C horizon, which includes an increasing proportion of rocks and fragments. In some soils the horizons are quite distinct, in others less so.

The A horizon, being nearest to the atmosphere, is more strongly weathered by the elements than the lower layers. The size of its soil particles tends to be reduced from that of sand to that of silt and clay. In time the small particles themselves may be decomposed and washed down to the B horizon by percolating water. Hence subsoils often contain an accumulation of dense fine clay. Sometimes a hardpan of impervious clay is formed which is not only an obstacle to cultivation, but results in the subsoil being poorly drained and aerated.

THE INFLUENCE OF CLIMATE AND RAINFALL

Different kinds of soil are the products of the varying influences of climate, vegetation and topography on the original parent material. The original material is broken down into fine particles and then, especially in hot wet climates, undergoes chemical changes which so transform it that soils formed under the same climatic conditions are often remarkably uniform, irrespective of the nature of the parent rocks. For this reason the world's soils can be divided into Great Soil Groups such as the red clay Latosols of the humid tropics, or the black Chernozems of the wheat belts of Russia and North America.

Surface soils and rocks are physically disintegrated by frost, heat, water and wind. In many areas they have also been ground down under the ice of glaciers. By these agencies particle size is reduced from that of stones and gravel to that of sand, silt and clay.

The fine clay particles are chemically reactive and chemical changes take place in the depths of the soil, mainly as a result of the solvent action of water. As water travels downwards through the soil it takes up carbon dioxide, and the carbonic and other acids dissolve the calcium, magnesium, sodium and potassium, which may then be washed out of the soil in the drainage water. This process, known as leaching, results in some of the soil's reserves of useful elements being lost. The amount of leaching depends on rainfall and temperature. In the humid tropics the useful cations are leached from the soil, leaving a residue of the less soluble elements such as iron and aluminium. Calcium and sodium are lost most rapidly, magnesium and potassium to a lesser extent. In drier climates on the other hand calcium is washed down only to the depth to which rain penetrates in the soil. The black soils of the steppes, for example, where the annual rainfall is only 10–20in, have a layer of accumulated calcium in the subsoil.

In humid climates everywhere, the soluble elements are leached away; the insoluble remain to form the soil. Hence in the temperate zones the relatively insoluble silica, iron and aluminium make up about 90 per cent of the soil. None of these is important in plant nutrition – although small amounts of iron are required. But the calcium, magnesium and potassium which tend to be lost are essential for plants, especially for the food plants on which man depends.

Leaching is most severe in porous sandy soils through which rain-water readily percolates. Clay soils on the other hand not only resist the rapid passage of water because of their greater density, but also hold calcium, magnesium and potassium against leaching.

The ability of clay soils to conserve these valuable elements can be explained by elementary chemical theory. Many compounds such as sodium, potassium, calcium and ammonium hydroxides, and sodium and potassium chlorides, separate into their constituent atoms or groups of atoms when dissolved in water. These separated atoms, called ions, are electrically charged. For example a solution of common salt in water does not contain molecules of sodium chloride, but sodium ions of positive charge, Na^+, and chloride ions of negative charge, Cl^-. The sodium atom loses an electron and becomes a positively charged sodium ion, the chlorine atom gains one electron and becomes a negatively charged chloride ion.

Ions which carry a positive electrical charge are called cations and those which carry a negative electrical charge are called anions. A cation tends to attract negatively charged ions, and an anion attracts positively charged ions. Clay particles, and also particles of organic matter, are predominantly negatively charged. They therefore tend to attract the cations of calcium, magnesium and potassium, and to hold them 'adsorbed' on their surfaces. These adsorbed cations are thus conserved as exchangeable ions, and can be taken up by the roots of plants. The less weathered clays of the temperate zones have a greater capacity for holding these cations than the more strongly weathered clays of the tropics.

NUTRIENT CYCLES

Climate largely determines vegetation, and in turn vegetation – trees and grasses – influence the physical and chemical structure of soils by leaf-fall and root residues. No true soil is without some organic matter.

In the most arid areas no plants will grow except cacti and other desert plants. Grasses usually predominate in areas of sparse rainfall, as savannahs and steppes, since grasses tolerate drought better than trees. Forests are the typical vegetation of humid climates, including the hardwoods of temperate climates and the conifers of cooler moist climates. Each predominant type of vegetation gives rise to typical soils and soil profiles. The natural grass areas, when broken for cultivation, yield black soils which are rich in organic matter, and are fertile because they are not strongly leached. In wetter climates the trees in their virgin state conserve and recycle nutrients. In forests the nutrients of the soil are continuously being recycled. Calcium and potassium are washed off leaf surfaces and return to the soil to be reabsorbed by roots. Leaves and litter fall to the ground and are decomposed by insects, bacteria and fungi, eventually releasing their store of nutrients for fresh use by plant roots; and dead roots similarly add organic matter to the soil. In tropical forests only the top few inches of soil may contain humus, the subsoils being infertile, and most of the available nutrients being in constant circulation. The amount of organic matter in soils, then, depends on the amount of vegetative cover, and on the rapidity with which plant remains are recycled. Grasses, as they have deep and extensive fibrous roots, leave more organic matter in subsoils than trees, whose leaf and litter layers may be confined to the top few inches of soil.

GREAT SOIL GROUPS

The influence of climate and vegetation on soil formation can be illustrated by considering some of the more important of the world's Great Soil Groups:

	Areas	Natural vegetation
Brown Earths	Much of Europe	Deciduous trees
Podsols	Northern latitudes	Conifers
Chernozems	Russian steppes	Grasses
Latosols	Tropical Africa and South America	Rain forest
Organic soils		Mosses

The Brown Earths, on which scientific agriculture began, were originally covered with deciduous forest. In their virgin state they have a surface layer rich in organic matter, underlain by a leached layer over a brown subsoil, which often contains more clay than the surface layers. They are permeable and reasonably fertile but their fertility tends to decline after some years of cultivation, when fertilisers, especially lime and phosphates, need to be supplied in order to maintain fertility.

Podsols are typically developed in cool moist climates, in sandy areas in which conifers predominate. An acid leaf litter falls to the surface and accumulates over a layer of thin black soil. Rain-water, which contains the acids of this top layer, washes down iron and aluminium from the A horizon to the B horizon, leaving a light ash-coloured sandy layer (the Russian *podsol* means ash) in the lower A horizon, from which the iron has been removed. The darker coloured material forms a dark-coloured layer in the B horizon.

Many podsols lie in northern latitudes where the growing season is short. They are acid, and usually require lime and fertilisers in large amounts.

Chernozems are black soils, rich in humus to a depth of 2ft or 3ft, derived from the tall grasses of the steppes and prairie. Beneath their deep topsoil is a layer of calcium carbonate which occurs at the depth to which winter rains penetrate. These soils develop in temperate climates in which the annual rainfall is limited to some 15–20in. The soil structure is excellent and the soils are of high fertility. The Chernozems are the great wheat-producing soils of the world, in North America, Argentina and the USSR. Crop production on these soils tends to be limited by lack of rainfall rather than by lack of soil minerals.

Latosols are the highly leached and weathered red soils of the tropics. Since in these latitudes the soil temperature is constantly high, chemical weathering takes place deep in the soil, so that it is often many feet deep. But as compared with the clays of temperate climates, they are acid, have a low cation-exchange capacity and cannot hold nutrient cations against leaching. Plants in these soils grow swiftly, and when they die they decay rapidly in the soil. Hence a continuous plant cover, everywhere desirable, is essential in these tropical soils if nutrients are not to be leached away.

Peat and fenland soils contain much organic matter. They are laid down originally in bogs and swamps where the soil is waterlogged. Water-plants, mosses, reeds and sedges grow, die and sink down under the water. The water shuts out the air so that plant remains are not oxidised and decomposed at the usual rate, but are partly preserved and decay very slowly into peat.

In areas of high rainfall the peat tends to be raw, undecomposed and acid. Where rainfall is less, peat soils have often been drained.

The entry of air and a supply of calcium in the ground water then create favourable conditions for the micro-organisms which decompose organic matter. Nitrogen is liberated, and these partially decomposed fen or 'muck' soils become highly productive, and are largely used for vegetable production. They are very retentive of water and their cation-exchange capacity is much higher than that of mineral soils. But some trace elements, especially copper and manganese, tend to be held in unavoidable form.

In most soils, then, except in arid or desert regions, nutrients can be leached away by high rainfall and organic matter lost as a result of rapid decomposition in high temperatures. Nutrients are conserved on the other hand by being held on the surface of clay particles and by being taken up and embodied in plant tissue. Some trees and plants are better at extracting and retaining soil minerals than others. Deciduous forests are heavy feeders on calcium and other cations, and their leaf-fall is high in these substances. Conifers by contrast are light feeders on bases, their leaf-fall is acid, and bases are not held but are leached from the soil. Grasses have deep and fibrous root systems which are replaced every few years. They contribute more organic matter to the deeper layers of soil than trees.

Plants and trees retard the loss of minerals from the soil, bring them to the surface and deposit them as organic residues. It is partly for this reason that the topsoil is more fertile than the subsoil. Grasses and trees, by retrieving nutrients from the subsoil, ensure the continuous circulation of valuable elements such as calcium, magnesium, potassium and phosphorus. But when grass or woodland is cleared and cropped, this self-sustaining cycle is broken, the fertility of the soil begins to decline and special measures have to be taken to replace the nutrients removed.

THE INFLUENCE OF TOPOGRAPHY

In wet climates the soils of mountains and uplands are poor and thin, while the soils of plains and valley bottoms are fertile and deep. On steep slopes, rainfall runs off the surface and washes away the finer particles of soil. Hence mountain slopes tend to be denuded of soil, or to be covered with only a few inches of soil over rock. Such soils are acid and heavily leached, and support only a heath type of vegetation. By contrast, in the bottoms and on the gentle slopes at the foot of steep hills, soil washed down from above tends to accumulate.

In a wet climate soluble elements in the soil are washed down and carried away in the drainage water. This is very evident in soils derived from limestone. In these soils the calcium carbonate is soluble in carbonated water and readily leached, only a little sand and clay residue being left behind to form a soil. Downland of pure chalk is often covered by just a few inches of red clay, which is the residue of many feet of chalk. Numerous soils derived from limestone may in fact be deficient in calcium carbonate in the topsoil.

SOIL TEXTURE

Soils are commonly classified as sands, silts or clays. And a good deal can be inferred about the productivity of a soil from its texture, that is the proportions of sand, silt and clay which it contains. Physically, soils contain particles of various sizes, varying from the large and visible particles of coarse sand to the minute and invisible particles of fine clay.

Most soils also contain stones, flints or fragments of rock. Although they make digging and cultivation more difficult, a certain proportion of stones, of the order of 10 per cent of the soil's volume, is an advantage. Stones improve the drainage of clays, make the soil warmer, and check evaporation during dry spells. But if stones or gravel make up a large part of the soil, clearly the soil will be poor and will not hold water.

By international convention soil particle sizes are classified as follows:

	Particle diameter limits in mm
Coarse sand	2–0·2
Fine sand	0·2–0·02
Silt	0·02–0·002
Clay	<0·002

Some idea of a soil's constituents can be obtained by shaking up a small amount of sieved soil in a bottle of water, and then leaving the mixture to settle. The larger sand particles quickly settle at the bottom, but the smaller particles take some hours to fall to the bottom. The soil particles are thus arranged in layers in order of their size, and the layers give an approximate measure of the amounts of sand, silt and clay in the soil.

Sandy soil is not all sand. Only on the most barren heath will the soil contain less than 10 per cent of clay and silt. Likewise no soils are pure clay but usually contain much fine sand or silt. Soils are commonly classified in a graduated sequence of texture from coarse sands to fine clays. The proportions of sand, silt and clay in some representative soil classes are illustrated in the diagram:

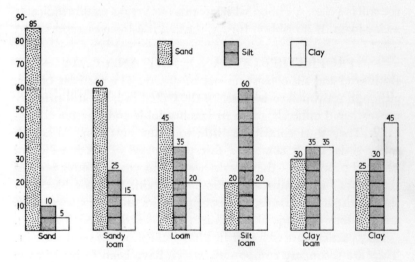

The composition of some soil classes

Sandy soils may contain 65 per cent or more of sand and very little clay. But even heavy clays seldom contain more than 50 per cent of true clay particles.

Sands tend to be infertile and droughty. Clays, although well supplied with nutrients, are cold, wet and difficult to cultivate. The intermediate loams are therefore generally to be preferred. But in most climates the most productive soils contain at least 20 per cent of clay.

Soil texture can be rapidly assessed by rubbing a sample of moist soil between thumb and finger. Sand feels gritty, silt smooth and silky, while clay is usually sticky and plastic. A more accurate tactile assessment can be made by moistening a small amount of soil until it adheres to itself. A loamy sand can then be compressed into a ball or rolled into a short cylinder, and will just retain its shape. A loam can be rolled out into a thin cylinder. A clay can not only be rolled into a thin cylinder, but the cylinder can be moulded into a circle.

Another test is to press some damp soil into a 'ribbon' between thumb and fingers. If a strong plastic ribbon can be easily formed the soil is a clay. A ribbon which forms but breaks readily indicates a clay loam. If no ribbon forms, the soil is a loam or sand.

PROPERTIES OF SAND, SILT AND CLAY

Both sand and silt consist mostly of quartz. The particles of silt, although too small to be seen by the naked eye, are still primary unweathered minerals, more or less insoluble and inactive chemically. They thus contribute little to plant nutrition. Although many soils which contain a fair percentage of silt have good physical properties – they retain water, but yet are better aerated than clays – some silts are difficult to drain. Silt may block up the pore spaces in sands, and because of its unstable structure be washed into drainage channels in the soil and impede drainage.

Clay particles are different in kind from those of sand and silt. They are secondary compounds which have been formed in the soil. Their crystal structure has only recently been revealed by X-ray diffraction studies. The minute particles – some 25,000 to the inch – are flat and have a characteristic lattice structure. The best known kinds of clay are kaolinite, illite and montmorillonite. The crystal units of kaolinite consist of silica and alumina sheets. Each unit is made up of a single sheet of silica linked with a single sheet of alumina. Hence kaolinite is said to have a 1:1 lattice structure.

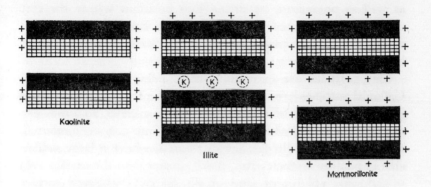

Structure of clay particles

The crystal units are strongly bonded by shared oxygen atoms. As a result, neither water nor ions can enter the space between the units, and the exchange capacity of kaolinite is confined to the edges of particles. Kaolin is the common form of clay found in the highly weathered soils of the tropics.

Montmorillonite particles are very much smaller, and their crystal units are less tightly bonded together. The crystal unit is a sheet of alumina sandwiched between two sheets of silica, and it is said to have a 2:1 lattice structure. The crystal units are only loosely bonded by weak oxygen linkages so that the interunit space is readily entered by water, cations and organic molecules. Montmorillonite thus expands on becoming wet and shrinks and cracks in drying.

Illite has the same type of crystal and the 2:1 lattice, but the crystal units are linked by potassium ions. The lattice does not therefore expand to the same extent as montmorillonite, and the cation-exchange capacity is less. Mica is another widely distributed type which has a structure similar to illite.

These three basic types of clay – kaolinite, montmorillonite and illite – are pure types which occur in varying proportions in clay soils. For example the clay fraction may consist of 60 per cent illite and 20 per cent kaolin, together with free iron and aluminium oxides. In some clays magnesium and ammonium ions as well as potassium, by fitting into positions within the clay crystal, can be retained within the particle. But these ions are not readily available to plants unless the particles are broken down by further weathering.

Clay particles are extremely small, being of colloidal size. Colloidal particles have diameters between 2 and 200 millimicrons (the millionth part of a metre). A millimicron is 10 times the angstrom unit, in which the size of atoms can be measured. Because of their colloidal size clay particles have a large surface area in relation to their mass, much greater than the surface area of the same volume of sand or silt. So clay has many surface atoms. These surface atoms are electrically unsatisfied. They therefore attract ions of opposite charge from the soil solution and hold them on their surfaces. Soil colloids are mostly negatively charged and tend accordingly to attract the positive ions (cations) calcium, magnesium and potassium. A typical clay particle may hold 20,000 cations on its surface in this way. This is one of the main reasons why clay soils are potentially more fertile than sands.

PROFILE CHARACTERISTICS

The soil profile gives useful information about the depth, texture, structure and drainage of a soil. The properties of the B horizon, or subsoil, are in many ways just as important as the properties of the topsoil. Usually topsoil and subsoil are of similar material. But sometimes a sandy or gravelly subsoil underlies a clay, and sometimes a clay soil underlies a sand or loam. A clay loam may lie over a stiff impervious clay, causing both A and B horizons to become waterlogged. On the other hand, a subsoil of coarse sand or gravel, such as occurs in heaths, results in a droughty and excessively drained soil. In woodlands a heavy retentive subsoil is often an advantage, provided drainage is adequate.

As a general rule the subsoil is relatively poor in organic matter and in soil micro-organisms, and is less fertile than the topsoil. When it is dry it tends to be harder than either the A horizon or the C horizon.

A heavy impervious clay will usually be obvious to inspection. The colour of the clay is a guide to the degree of aeration. Red or brown clays are usually well aerated; blue-grey or mottled clays are not. In the red-brown clays the iron in the soil is in the ferric form. When there is little air in the soil the iron is reduced to the ferrous state, only one atom of iron being combined with each oxygen atom. When this occurs, the subsoil appears blue-grey and is likely to be poorly drained.

A subsoil may be so poorly drained in winter that it is unsuitable for perennials, but it may dry out in the spring and summer to allow annuals to be grown.

In order to get some idea of the drainage status of a soil, holes 2–3ft deep may be dug and filled with water. If all the water drains away within an hour or two, drainage is adequate. If there is still water in the holes after twenty-four hours, drainage is obviously imperfect.

Inspection of the soil profile should suggest what can be done to improve the soil and the kind of crops that are likely to do best on it. In a very shallow soil, gardening may have to be confined to annual flowers or shallow-rooting vegetables. If the soil is also of poor quality, or if the topsoil has been removed, the only remedy is to bring in loads of good topsoil. About 1 ton is required for every 5sq yd to provide a depth of 6–7in of soil. Bringing in topsoil need not be prohibitively expensive in areas in which a good loam is readily available. Indeed in many new housing estates it is standard practice to bring in topsoil to spread on new gardens.

If the texture and structure of the A and B horizons are unpromising, the remedy is to bring in farmyard manure, to dig in composts and green manures, or to put down the land to grasses and clovers for a year or two. If the soil is a sand which drains too readily, it should not be left bare but filled with cover crops whose roots will prevent leaching.

Poor drainage is perhaps the condition which is hardest to set right. Drains may be laid or soakaways constructed through impervious layers. Layers of coarse gravel may be laid down underneath the topsoil. Failing all else, plants can be grown which do not mind a wet soil. Not many plants like to have 'wet feet', but there are some which will grow in wet soils – among the trees are willows, alders and some poplars, for example. Currants and gooseberries will tolerate a wetter soil than more other bush fruits. Among ornamental plants ivy and philodendron are fairly tolerant of wet conditions. Annual flowers can also be grown, provided the soil dries out in the spring and summer.

If topsoil and subsoil are markedly different in colour and texture, the subsoil should not be brought to the surface or mixed in with the top layers. The natural topsoil will be more fertile than the subsoil, containing more nutrients and more soil microorganisms, and it will usually be more open and better aerated. The subsoil on the other hand will usually have less nutrients and a poorer structure; and raw clay subsoils may be toxic to young seedlings, since they may contain reduced forms of iron and manganese. The reduced forms are more soluble than the oxidised forms, and so may be present in such large quantities as to be toxic to young plants.

It is not always of advantage to increase the depth of cultivation. Deep cultivation by trenching is likely to be useful only where a hardpan or impervious layer is limiting the root zone. The aim in trenching such stiff subsoils is to extend the topsoil and the feeding zone of plants. Merely to break up the subsoil is nearly always ineffective. Manure and organic material need to be buried in the subsoil if the improvement in structure is not to be merely temporary. Improvement can also be effected by green manuring with deep-rooted annuals whose roots, when they decay, leave channels in the subsoil.

CHAPTER 3

WATER, AIR
AND SOIL STRUCTURE

Where now the vital energy that moved,
While Summer was, the pure and subtle lymph
Through the imperceptible meandering veins
Of leaf and flower?

(Cowper)

It is common knowledge that plants need much water: water makes up about four-fifths of their weight. But it is not so commonly known that nearly all of the water which plants absorb from the soil is lost into the atmosphere through transpiration (evaporation from the leaf). For water is supplied in visible liquid form, but escapes in the invisible form of water vapour. A plant can be likened to a wick through which water is drawn up from the soil and evaporated into the air. Water is also the medium through which mineral nutrients are absorbed from the soil, and the solvent for the carbon dioxide and oxygen of the air. It keeps the guard cells of the stomata turgid, so that the stomata remain open and photosynthesis can proceed.

As a result of transpiration, a plant must take up between 200 and 1,000 parts of water for every part of its dry matter. During the growing season a high proportion of the rainfall is lost in this way. Even in humid climates summer transpiration may exceed summer rainfall, thus checking growth. And, taken the world over, shortage of water more frequently limits plant growth than any other cause.

Transpiration is greatest when the weather is hot and dry,

49

and least when it is cool and moist. In hot weather, when transpiration exceeds water uptake, plants wilt and may even die. Since plants make their main growth during the warmer seasons when evaporation from the soil is also greatest, the amount of summer rainfall is clearly vital and of critical importance to those vegetables and crops which are adapted to rapid growth under moist conditions. But the native vegetation of dry areas has evolved various means of conserving water. Such plants have only small leaves or develop spines, eg gorse. Cacti have thick leaves in which water is stored. Australian eucalypts turn their leaves edgewise to the sun, thus reducing transpiration. And many plants which grow on dry banks, such as thyme and marjoram, exude aromatic oils which reduce the loss of water.

The amount of precipitation (rainfall, snow, etc) together with its seasonal distribution, largely determines the type of vegetation. In the ever-recurring water cycle, rainfall either evaporates and returns to the atmosphere or passes through the soil to streams and oceans, from which it may once more be evaporated.

About half the rainfall is lost to plants. In heavy storms of rain, all the water cannot infiltrate into the soil but runs off the surface of the ground. There is also constant evaporation of water from the surface soil to the atmosphere, particularly in hot dry climates. And, finally, in humid climates water percolates down into the soil beyond the plant root zones and is lost in drainage water.

The rate at which water can enter a soil depends on the soil's texture and structure. Sandy, gravelly or stony soils readily admit water, as do the tropical latosols which have deep profiles of non-expanding clay. In heavy clays which swell on becoming wet, on the other hand, cracks and openings in the soil close up, the surface becomes packed and a continuous sheet of water builds up on the surface. Each soil has an infiltration capacity, the amount of rain which it can absorb in a given time. If a soil's infiltration capacity is 0·25in per hour and 1in of rain falls in an hour, 75 per cent of the rain will not be absorbed but will accumulate on the surface or run off if the ground is sloping.

Page *51* Legume roots showing the nodules of nitrogen-fixing bacteria. (*Above*) Soya bean; (*below*) runner bean

COMPLETE | NO Na | NO₂S | NO Mg | NO P | NO Fe | NO Ca | NO K | NO N

Fig. 53. Disparity of growth among bean plants grown in various nutrient solutions

The rate of percolation through soil likewise depends on texture and structure, being rapid through open sandy soils and much slower in clays. As fine clay often accumulates in the B horizon, the downward movement of water is therefore slowed down, so that the topsoil can become waterlogged even when the deeper subsoil may be free-draining.

After percolating down through the soil by gravity, water

The water cycle

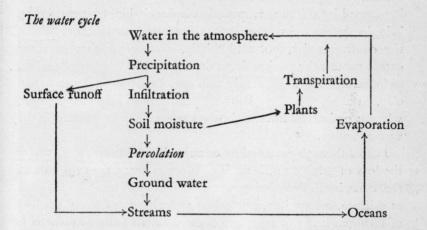

reaches the water table, at which the soil is completely saturated. In wet climates a deep hole dug in the ground will reach this level of ground water. In river valleys or near ponds or lakes the water table is usually only a few feet below the soil surface. In such places water may rise by capillarity and be reached by deep-rooting plants. But in most soils the ground water is too far below the surface for this small capillary rise to be of use to plants. In most areas, and certainly in dry areas, rainfall percolating through or stored in the soil is the only important source of soil moisture.

Water, then, is lost to plants through runoff, surface evaporation and percolation below the root zone. The overland flow of water in runoff is perhaps the greatest and most avoidable source of loss. The overland flow tends to wash away valuable clay and

D

humus, and to erode the soil. Runoff is greatest on bare soils, and is lessened by plant cover. The soil surface can also be protected by mulches or crop residues left on the surface. Maintaining a good soil structure, by digging in manures and plant residues, also helps to keep the soil open and to maintain the infiltration rate. On sloping ground, contour ridges prevent surface runoff during heavy rains.

Surface evaporation is not readily prevented. When moist soil is warmed by the sun, evaporation is inevitable. Cultivation, by bringing moist soil to the surface, increases evaporation. Where the climate is dry, hot and windy, surface mulches to some extent protect the surface from drying out. In very dry climates, as in parts of Australia, sandy soils may be more productive than clay. In sandy soil, light showers penetrate swiftly into the soil, whereas on heavier soil the showers are quickly evaporated in the surface inches.

Losses through percolation occur only in wet climates, where the loss of soluble nutrients is of more concern than the loss of the water itself. Percolating water takes with it soluble salts such as calcium, magnesium, potassium and nitrate nitrogen, the loss of nitrogen being of especial concern. Loss of these nutrients is greater in open sandy soils than in clays.

THE WATER CONTENT OF SOILS

Soils differ in their capacity to retain moisture. Sands retain little water and are droughty. Clays and organic soils are more retentive; in fact the water-holding capacity of a soil depends on its clay and humus content.

It is useful to distinguish the water content of soils when they are 'oven-dry', at wilting-point, at field capacity and at saturation.

State of soil	*Form of water*
'Oven-dry'	Hygroscopic – unavailable
Between permanent wilting-point and field capacity	Available to plants
Saturated	Excess water drained away

In the laboratory the 'oven-dry' weight of a soil is determined by drying a sample to 105° C. The percentage of water present in various states of wetness can then be expressed in relation to this 'oven-dry' weight.

The permanent wilting-point is found by growing a test plant in the soil until it wilts and will not recover from wilting unless more water is added. The amount of moisture still present in the soil but unavailable to the plant is then determined.

A soil is at field capacity after a day or so of heavy rain. Field capacity indicates the amount of water which is retained in the network of soil pores against drainage by gravity and it can be measured roughly by weighing out some 'oven-dry' soil in a perforated tin, soaking the soil and leaving it to drain, and then reweighing it.

The only water which plants can use is that held between wilting-point and field capacity. Below wilting-point the soil moisture is held so tightly that plant roots cannot draw it out of the soil. Above field capacity excess water drains away into the soil below the root zone.

The graph on p56 shows that the available water in the sandy loam is considerably less than that in the clay loam.

Field capacity depends largely on the size of the spaces between soil particles. The smaller the pore, the more tightly it holds water. A sandy soil has few small capillary pores and thus a low water-holding capacity. Loams and clays have many fine capillary pores in the soil crumbs, together with larger pores in between the crumbs. The capillary pores still hold water at field capacity, while the larger pores fill with air.

But all the advantage does not lie with the heavier soils. In light soils roots penetrate more deeply and extensively than in clays, and can thus reach moisture at deeper levels. And lighter soils yield up moisture more readily; whereas in clays there is much 'dead' unavailable water. The strength with which water is held in the soil increases enormously as the soil dries out. It is therefore necessary to use a logarithmic scale, the pF scale, running from 0 to 7, to measure the force of retention. The scale values represent the logarithm of the height of a column of water in centimetres, which exerts the same pull as the soil exerts on its water. For example, pF3 indicates that the soil water is

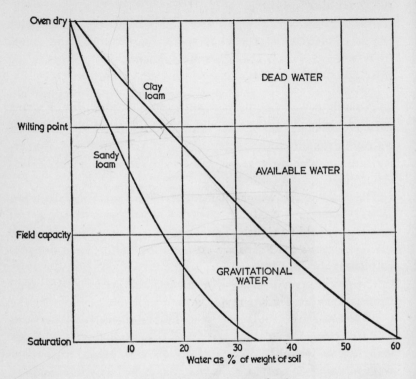

Available water in two types of soil

under the tension exerted by a column of 10^3cm of water – which is roughly equivalent to the height held up by the pressure of one atmosphere. The wilting-point lies at about pF4·2 and field capacity at around pF2·5 or one-third atmosphere. In the laboratory these pressures can be applied to soils in a compressed-air chamber.

THE PRACTICE OF WATERING

In hot weather, growing plants need about 1in of water every ten days, rather less in dull weather. The reserve of moisture in the soil may be insufficient. The following table indicates the reserve of available moisture in differing soils:

Soil type	Available water in inches per foot depth
Sand	$\frac{1}{2}$–$\frac{3}{4}$in
Loam	$1\frac{1}{4}$–$1\frac{3}{4}$in
Clay	2in

A sandy soil of depth 2ft could supply only 1–1$\frac{1}{2}$in of water. So if no rain falls, water would have to be supplied every ten

Saturation — Pore space full of water, air excluded

Field capacity — A film of water surrounds soil particles. Pore space contains air

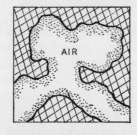

Wilting point — The little water that remains is unavailable

A soil pore under different conditions of moisture

days in order to keep plants growing. A deep clay soil on the other hand would yield a good deal more water, assuming that plant roots go deep enough into the soil.

Seedlings and shallow-rooted plants suffer from drought more than mature plants which can reach subsoil water. If the spring and early summer months are dry, watering of young plants becomes essential. Shallow-rooted plants, which suffer first in drought and respond quickly to water, include annual flowers, lettuce, onions, potatoes and brassicas.

Plants which require a good supply of moisture if they are to do well include among shrubs the rhododendron; among soft fruits, blackcurrants and raspberries; and among vegetables, lettuce, cauliflower, celery, early potatoes and rhubarb.

There is little basis for the common belief that once frequent watering has been started it must be continued, except perhaps in very sandy or stony unretentive soils. In such soils shallow watering may result in shallow root systems confined to the top-soil, which then rapidly dries out unless watering is frequent. Watering should always be deep and thorough, wetting the root zone to full capacity, which needs perhaps 1–2in of water. Now 1in of water is about 4½gal per sq yd. Evidently the watering-can needs to be replaced by the hose and sprinkler or, better, by a perforated plastic hose. A ½in hose and sprinkler will usually deliver 3–4gal per min. If it covers 20sq yd it will therefore need to run for about 30min to deliver 1in of water (90gal) to the area. A gentle spray or layflat hose giving about ½in of water per hour does less damage to soil structure. There is of course no point in giving more water at a time than the soil will retain, but frequent shallow watering which wets only the surface soil should be avoided.

If a hot sun is shining, watering overhead by sprinkler should be done in the evening. The dangers of leaf scorch have been much exaggerated, but it is more economical to water in the evening. Water can be given to the roots at any time. In dry weather, furrows can be made along the rows or circular basins dug around shrubs.

Ways of reducing the need for watering include:

1 making garden-beds deep, if necessary excavating and filling in with good soil. Beds may also be raised 6in above the surface;

2 digging in humus-forming substances such as farmyard manure, composts, plant remains, peat;

3 planting in autumn or early winter rather than in spring. This applies particularly to roses, lilies, carnations, irises, etc and to flowering shrubs;

4 when plants are established, using surface mulches of grass cuttings, compost or peat. To avoid the appearance of untidiness, mulches can be forked in lightly and covered with soil.

SOIL AIR

Of all the essentials for plant growth, the oxygen of the soil air is the element which is perhaps the least obvious to the human senses, and the one most likely to be overlooked. Many people have indeed learnt from sad experience that pot plants can be killed by 'over-watering' – that is, by keeping the soil so saturated with moisture that nearly all the soil air is expelled.

A clod of soil, which feels so solid, contains about as much air and water as solid matter. Air and water are held in the pore spaces between the solid particles, and in the minute passages and fissures which cannot be seen with the naked eye. As water moves into the soil, air is forced out, so that the amount of the one is inversely related to the amount of the other. If a pot of soil is immersed in water, the soil air can be seen to bubble to the surface, and in much the same way air is displaced from the soil by heavy rains. Then as the water drains away, or is transpired, air again enters the soil pores. If the soil contains plenty of large pores, these will still hold air even when the soil is very wet. But if it is compacted and poorly drained, the pores may stay full of water so that air cannot re-enter the soil.

Since plant roots need oxygen, the soil must contain enough pore space to admit air; and further, since the soil's oxygen is continuously being depleted, the system of pores must connect with the atmosphere so that the soil can be ventilated and the oxygen renewed. In stiff clays this may not happen. Their fine network of capillary pores may be partially isolated from the surface air, and there may be many blocked pores which are

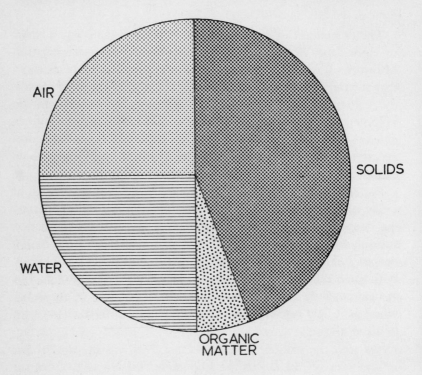

The composition of moist soil

not connected to other pore spaces. In compact soils, obviously, the deeper the soil layer the less well it is ventilated, unless the subsoil contains cracks and fissures, earthworm holes or channels left by decayed roots.

A clay soil of poor structure may have only 10 per cent of air space. A loam soil of good structure has more adequate space for air and water.

Soil air contains less oxygen and more carbon dioxide than atmospheric air. Typical percentages by volume for the composition of soil and surface air are:

	O_2	CO_2	N_2
Surface air	20·97	0·03	79
Soil air	20·65	0·25	79·1

The percentage of carbon dioxide in the soil tends to be seven or eight times as high as in the outside air. This accumulation of carbon dioxide does not have the adverse effect on plant roots that it would have on animals. But in the deeper layers of the soil the volume of carbon dioxide may be actually greater than the volume of oxygen and, under these conditions, when the soil air contains less than 10 per cent of oxygen, roots cannot function effectively. Hence, apart from the mechanical impedance, roots cannot penetrate compact subsoils for lack of oxygen.

For example, walnut trees were found to make poor growth in a clay which had a heavy airless subsoil, hardly any roots penetrating deeper than 3ft. But in a silt loam which had a well-aerated subsoil, the greater part of the root system was growing in the deeper soil layers and extended down to more than 10ft. Now both these soils had about the same capacity to supply water, but at field capacity the clay contained only 5 per cent of air at 3ft, whereas at field capacity the silt loam contained over 25 per cent of air at 3ft.

THE NEED FOR OXYGEN

In the absence of oxygen all the vital functions of plants cease. Although the most obvious work of plants – lifting water from the soil – depends upon the energy of the sun, plants also need energy for intracellular chemical reactions. The energy for these reactions comes from respiration. In respiration energy is derived from the oxidation of sugars:

$$C_6H_{12}O_6 + 6O_2 \rightarrow 6CO_2 + 6H_2O + \text{energy}$$

All parts of the plant respire: leaves, fruits, stems and roots.

Hence roots cannot either grow or take up water in the absence of oxygen, and indeed will wilt when standing in waterlogged soil. Oxygen is also needed by the aerobic soil microbes. The more actively plants are growing and the more active are the soil microbes, the more oxygen is consumed and the more carbon dioxide is produced. Thus there is an inverse relation between the oxygen and carbon dioxide percentages, oxygen decreasing as carbon dioxide increases.

All the constituents of the air are important to plants. Oxygen is needed for respiration. The carbon dioxide in the soil is dissolved by water to produce carbonic acid. This in turn helps to dissolve minerals so that they become more available to plants in the soil solution. Though not of major importance, carbon dioxide may also be reabsorbed at the surface of the soil, passing into the leaves and being used in photosynthesis. The nitrogen gas of the soil air is used by some of the soil and root-nodule bacteria to produce the combined nitrogen that plant roots can assimilate.

It may seem anomalous that, although plants die in waterlogged soils for lack of oxygen, they nevertheless can be grown in water cultures. When plants are grown in a bottle of water, the roots obtain oxygen from the small amount of oxygen which is dissolved in the water and instantly renewed from the atmosphere at the water surface. And, as the roots develop, air has to be blown through the water every day to renew the supply of oxygen and to remove carbon dioxide. Also, an air space is maintained between the root crown and the water surface. If the root crown is submerged, the plant will die just as it does in waterlogged soil. This is true of most land plants. In water plants such as willow, rice, cat's-tail, etc, oxygen can diffuse down from their aerial parts to their roots. Other plants, including the philodendrons and ivies often raised as house plants, can be grown in water, although they make better growth in soil. In fact different kinds of plants vary in their oxygen requirements. Among those which have high oxygen requirements and therefore do better on lighter, more open soils, are potatoes, tomatoes, peas and most fruit-trees. Grasses on the other hand are less demanding, and trees such as planes and limes, which are frequently used for street-planting, can grow in soil which is covered with paving and therefore poorly ventilated.

Oxygen is likewise essential for the germination of most seeds. The energy which is required to start growth is provided by the oxidation of the seed's reserves of food substances. During germination the rate of respiration and oxygen uptake increase. Hence seeds will not germinate if a hard crust forms on the surface of the seed bed, preventing oxygen from entering the soil, nor will they germinate if the seed bed is so wet that the pore spaces are full of water. Therefore seed composts contain peat and a mixture of grit and coarse sand which, while retaining adequate moisture, also drain well and continue to have an open structure. Similarly most cuttings root better in a mixture of sand and peat than in sand alone, because peat, as well as retaining more moisture, contains about twice as much air as does sand.

Again, the root growth of plants grown in porous earthenware pots tends to be close against the side of the pot where the soil is well aerated. But in plastic pots the soil is less well aerated, and water is not lost from the side of the pot. It is therefore easy to over-water young plants in plastic pots. The peat mixture becomes saturated with water and airless, growth ceases, and the plant yellows and often dies.

ENSURING THE AERATION OF SOILS

For optimum growth the air should fill about one-third of the total pore space. In medium and heavy soils it is frequently present in lesser quantity, and more air is nearly always desirable. In lighter soils, on the other hand, too much air can be present, leading to excessively rapid oxidation of organic matter and to the drying out of the soil. Excessive aeration may occur when sandy or peaty soils are over-cultivated. Aeration can be reduced by mulching the surface.

But excess aeration is a lesser problem than inadequate aeration. Inadequate aeration is common in wet clay soils and subsoils, particularly if they have been trampled or compacted. This is another way of saying that such soils are poorly drained. They are poorly drained because, although they may have a large total volume of pore space, the pore diameters are so small that water remains in them after rain, and air is excluded. Desirably, part of the total pore space should still hold air when the soil is at its field capacity for water. Air will enter the soil at field capacity, provided that pore diameters are of the order of 50-75 microns. In order to bring this about, the soil needs to contain plenty of aggregates above 0·25mm in size. Anything which reduces the size of the soil aggregates below this reduces the aeration porosity of the soil.

Aeration porosity is reduced by over-watering, by cultivating the soil when it is too wet, by compacting or trampling, by leaving the soil surface bare so that it is broken down by rain and crusted over, and by failure to ensure adequate organic matter in the soil. There has been concern in recent years that the structure and porosity of some agricultural soils have deteriorated for these reasons.

Aeration porosity can be increased by drainage, by timely cultivation, by breaking up clay subsoils, by planting deep-rooting crops, and by vertical mulching (digging organic residues into slits cut into the subsoil); and by growing cover crops and green manures, by digging in crop residues and farmyard manure, and in general by building up humus in the soil.

SOIL STRUCTURE

In brief, the plants' needs for water and air are best met when the soil has a continuous system of pores right down from its surface to the lower layers, through which surplus water can drain while the soil air is constantly renewed from the external air. These conditions are met when the soil has a granular or crumb structure. Structure refers to the arrangement of soil particles into larger aggregates.

In a pure sand the individual grains are not bound together or aggregated and the soil is very compact. But when clay and humus are present they bind the soil particles into aggregates which vary in size from sand grains to large clods. When soil is in the crumb condition it can be likened to well-baked bread which contains many air spaces.

The advantages of a crumb structure are that fine particles are

Root growth of plants in uncompacted (*left*) and compacted (*right*) sandy loam

held within the crumb and do not block the drainage pores. And since the crumbs are irregular in shape, spaces remain between them into which air can diffuse. Also the crumbs themselves are porous.

In the top soil the best crumb size is thought to lie in the range 0·5–5mm, more towards the smaller limit in dry conditions and towards the larger limit in wet conditions – that is, crumb size should lie between that of sand and gravel. This is the kind of crumb size which gardeners try to produce in a fine seed bed, as for onions. The fine crumb structure then allows seeds to be sown at a uniform depth, and ensures that the soil crumbs will fit closely around the seed to keep it moist, while at the same time allowing air to circulate so that oxygen is available for germination.

After cultivation, when a good tilth has been obtained, seed beds need to be consolidated so that their surface will not dry out. This is usually accomplished by trampling over the soil

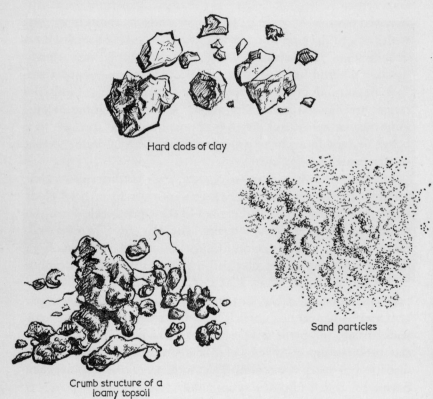

Hard clods of clay

Sand particles

Crumb structure of a
loamy topsoil

Examples of soil aggregates

with a scuffling motion of the boot so as to make the surface uniformly firm; or by using a light roller. Consolidation is adequate when the surface soil can be pushed down only slightly with a clenched fist. Most soils need to be consolidated very soon after cultivation, and before any subsequent rain.

It is not of course sufficient to ensure a good structure in the top few inches of soil only. Water should be absorbed and air should circulate in the subsoil also. The subsoil should therefore have plenty of middle-sized aggregates (about 5mm across), so that passages are left through which water and air can move. Some subsoils have a block structure produced by both horizontal and vertical cracking; others a columnar structure with pronounced vertical cracking. The most difficult subsoils to deal with contain deep and impervious layers of clay which have no definite lines of cleavage. Water percolates only very slowly through such subsoils, air cannot enter and roots cannot penetrate.

A dense and poorly aerated subsoil often defeats both the farmer and the gardener. The results of deep ploughing or digging may be ephemeral unless it is possible to cut through to a better drained layer, or to provide some system of drains so that surplus water can get away.

In addition to the size of aggregates, their hardness and water-stability are also important. Soils should not form hard clods when they dry out, but neither should the clods break down too readily on becoming moist again. The clay fraction of a soil, more than any other factor, brings about the aggregation of particles. A lump of dry clay soil may be so hard that it cannot be broken by hand. When it is moist, containing say about 30 per cent moisture, it can be crumbled easily. If between 30 per cent and 50 per cent of water is added, the clay becomes a plastic sticky paste, and if the water is increased to over 50 per cent the clay becomes liquid. When a clay soil is wet, its clay particles are dispersed in water suspension. The sand and silt particles are then covered with the film of clay in colloidal suspension, which acts as a cement. Thus a heavy clay, if worked or trampled on when wet, sets to a massive state on drying, the colloidal suspension filling up the pore spaces. Clay pastes are of course used in pottery, in brickmaking and for waterproofing the bottoms of ponds. Just how heavy or difficult a clay is will depend on the percentage of clay in the soil, on the fineness of the particles and on the type of clay. Soils which contain more than 35 per cent of clay are usually unsuitable for horticulture in temperate regions.

On the other hand, soils containing from 12 per cent to 35 per cent of clay can normally retain a structure, provided they are cultivated when they hold the appropriate degree of moisture.

A more desirable kind of cementing agent however is not pure clay but a complex of clay and humus, and especially one which contains lime. If a clod of good topsoil from a clay loam is viewed under a magnifying glass, lines of cleavage can be seen within the larger whole, as well as the dead plant roots and other organic matter which divide the soil mass so that it shatters easily into smaller units.

Lime itself has a mellowing effect on clay, causing the clay particles to cling together or flocculate into groups. But these groups are still only of about silt size, so that they need to be further aggregated if they are to provide favourable conditions for plant roots. This further aggregation, in the presence of humus rich in lime, appears to be the work of the minute soil fungi and bacteria which in decomposing the organic matter produces substances which bind the flocculated clay into larger crumbs.

There are always many soil micro-organisms near plant roots. Grass roots, for example, when lifted gently from the soil, will have adhering to them many clusters of soil crumbs. It is thought that the microscopic organisms surrounding the roots bind soil particles into granules, which are then held together in clusters by the root hairs. Hence soil that has been under grass usually has a good granulated structure, and the most effective way of restoring soil structure is to put land down to grass.

SOIL DENSITY

A loose friable soil has a low weight per unit volume, while a dense compacted soil has a high weight per unit volume. The specific gravity of the solid fraction of mineral soils is about 2·6; that is, a compact mass of soil particles weighs 2·6 times an equal volume of water. This is referred to as the particle density of the soil. But a block of soil taken from the ground will have only about half this density, since the volume of the block contains only about half solids, the other half being space filled with air or water. The actual volume weight of a soil is referred to as the bulk density. Bulk density is determined by dividing the weight of a block of 'oven-dry' soil in grammes by its volume in cubic centimetres.

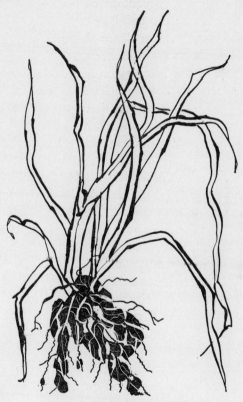

Soil granules adhering to roots

In practice bulk density is measured by thrusting a metal cylinder of known volume into the ground so that it is filled with soil. The sample of soil is taken from the cylinder, dried and weighed. Its weight in grammes is then divided by the volume of the cylinder in cubic centimetres. Bulk-density values range from about 1·6 for sands to 1·0 or less for clays.

E

The total pore space as such gives little indication of the working qualities of a soil since clays, which are difficult to work, have much pore space while sands, which are easier, have less. In practice it is more important to know whether the pores are large enough to admit the passage of air and water. Nevertheless, within a soil class, the percentage of pore space gives a useful measure of how friable the soil is.

Subsoils are always more dense than surface soils – and old garden soils are always more dense and compacted than virgin soils – unless they have been given large quantities of farmyard manure, crop residues, etc. And when soils are trampled or compacted by the wheels of machines, not only does their bulk density rise but the proportion of large pores in the pore space is reduced, thus impeding drainage and aeration.

CULTIVATION

It is often recommended that clay soils should be left rough-dug over winter to allow frost to shatter the clods. But research has shown that frost action improves structure only when freezing is gradual and the soil is moist but not wet. Under these conditions part of the soil remains unfrozen but is compressed by the expansion of the frozen parts, resulting in stable, compressed aggregates of a suitable size. But the rapid freezing and thawing of wet soil causes uniform icing throughout the soil. This results in a breaking apart and dispersion of soil aggregates. Large clods may indeed be broken down but the new smaller aggregates are unstable. Where winters are mild it is evident that exposing clay to frost action may produce a good spring tilth, but that in harder continental-type winters frost action, although breaking larger clods, may also destroy the bonds which hold smaller aggregates together. And the structure of sandy soils is also liable to be damaged by frost.

Clay crumbs naturally tend to form aggregates after cycles of moisture and drying out. The swelling and shrinking of the colloids cracks the soil. Then, as the soil dries out, the strong adhesive properties of the colloids bind the soil into clods.

If clay is dug when it is too dry it breaks into large hard clods, which then shatter into fine particles and dust. If it is dug when too wet it falls into compact layers, which again break down into hard clods on drying. For every soil there is an optimum point, usually around 35 per cent moisture, at which cultivation will leave the soil with a good structure – provided organic matter and lime status are also adequate.

SYNTHETIC SOIL CONDITIONERS

Since it was discovered that the soil micro-organisms, in decomposing organic matter, produce polysaccharide gums which bind the soil particles together, chemists have attempted to make synthetic compounds which would act in the same way. Polyvinyl compounds such as IBMA and VAMA (the ammonium salt of isobutylenemaleic acid copolymer, and vinylacetate maleic acid) have proved to have good soil-aggregating properties, and they are not broken down by soil bacteria like most sorts of organic matter.

It is claimed that these conditioners, when mixed with the soil in quantities of only about 0·05 per cent of the soil's weight, produce as much soil aggregation as much larger quantities of organic residues. The improvement of physical structure is greatest on clay soils. They are not substitutes for organic matter and they add no plant nutrients to the soil. But by improving the porosity and aeration of the soil they may enable roots to develop more rapidly, and thus draw on a greater volume of soil for water and nutrients.

The high cost of the synthetic conditioners has restricted their use. And, as often happens, exaggerated claims by advertisers perhaps led to unreasonable expectations of their merits.

CHAPTER 4

ESSENTIAL NUTRIENTS

The soil must be renewed which, often washed,
Loses its treasure of salubrious salts,
And disappoints the roots

(Cowper)

The earth's crust consists for the most part of oxygen, silicon, aluminium and iron. But these elements, which together make up about 90 per cent of most mineral soils, are of little importance in plant nutrition, and form the mere skeleton of the soil. The rest of the earth's crust is mostly calcium, magnesium, potassium and sodium. These elements, which are strongly basic, are of primary importance in nutrition. Finally, making up barely 2 per cent of the total are the eighty or so other elements, some of which, in small amounts, are essential for plant growth.

Most soils are formed not of free elements, but of complex aluminium and iron silicates of the four strong bases: calcium, magnesium, potassium and sodium. But these silicates vary greatly in form and chemical composition.

At least sixteen elements are essential for higher plants: carbon, hydrogen, oxygen, nitrogen, phosphorus, potassium, calcium, magnesium, sulphur, iron, manganese, copper, zinc, boron, molybdenum and chlorine. Cobalt is also required by legumes. Other elements such as sodium and silicon are beneficial to some plants, but not essential to them. In addition, many other elements are present in plant material; indeed some mystics believe that all the elements are present in all living material and are essential to life. Certainly traces of some twenty or thirty other elements are commonly found in plants. Some of them such as arsenic, chromium, nickel and lead are harmful. But most such as rubidium, silver, gold, tin and titanium are of unknown significance, and are thought to be present only incidentally. A few plants are known to accumulate certain metals, and can be used by mineral prospectors as indicators of high concentrations of precious metals in the soil.

About 95 per cent of the substance of plants is made of the lighter elements, oxygen, carbon and hydrogen, which are derived from air and water. In photosynthesis the sugars are made from carbon dioxide and water. These sugars are then elaborated into starches, fats and proteins in complicated series of chemical reactions. These reactions are controlled and speeded up by enzymes – organic catalysts of which there are some hundreds in each plant cell.

Proteins, for example, are built up from amino-acids such as glycine which contains both nitrogen and carbohydrate. The nitrogen has to be absorbed from the soil by the roots. In the same way other mineral nutrients are needed, both to combine with the carbon compounds and to act as catalysts. Large quantities of those elements such as nitrogen which are the constituents of plant substance, are required.

Each element has many functions. Magnesium, for example, is a constituent of chlorophyll, but it is also active in enzyme systems. Similarly nitrogen, as well as being a constituent of the cell nucleus, is involved in all enzyme systems. Besides such major elements, smaller quantities of minor or trace elements are required, many of them heavier metallic substances such as iron, copper and zinc. These trace elements act mostly as catalysts or activators of the chemical transformations which take place within plant cells.

There are twelve essential nutrients, taken up from the soil, which are of importance. Six are referred to as major elements, being for the most part actual constituents of plant substance and therefore required in large amounts; and six are referred to as minor or trace elements which, being mostly enzyme constituents and enzyme activators, are needed in much smaller amounts, but are nevertheless just as essential as the major elements.

These elements and the main forms in which they are absorbed by plant roots are:

Major elements			Minor elements		
Nitrogen	N	NO_3^- (nitrate) or NH_4^+ (ammonium)			
Phosphorus	P	$H_2PO_4^-$, HOP_4^{--}	Iron	Fe	Fe^{++}
			Manganese	Mn	Mn^{++}
Potassium	K	K^+	Boron	B	$H_2BO_3^-$
Calcium	Ca	Ca^{++}	Zinc	Zn	Zn^{++}
Magnesium	Mg	Mg^+	Copper	Cu	Cu^{++}
Sulphur	S	SO_4^{--}	Molybdenum	Mo	MoO_4^{--}

In the solid material of the soil these elements are contained in compound substances. But in the soil solution, compounds tend to separate into their component ions – that is, into atoms or molecules which carry positive or negative electric charges. For example, common salt in solution separates into a positively charged sodium ion or cation, Na^+, and a negatively charged chlorine ion or anion, Cl^-. It is in the form of ions that plant roots absorb the essential nutrients.

Among the essential elements the base-forming elements, or cations, include ammonium, potassium, calcium and magnesium, together with the minor cations iron, manganese, zinc and copper. The acid-forming elements, or anions, include nitrate, phosphorus and sulphur, and the minor elements boron and molybdenum.

The essential elements can be shown to be essential by growing plants in water or in sand cultures, and supplying all the necessary elements except one. In water culture the plant is supported in a glass jar which contains the nutrient solution. The oxygen required by the roots is supplied by forcing a stream of air through the solution at intervals.

In sand or gravel cultures the plant is grown in inert sand or gravel which provides mechanical support but does not supply nutrients. The nutrient solution is then supplied by drip or by irrigation. By such methods plant physiologists had already established by the middle of the last century that the major elements and iron were essential. The other minor elements were not

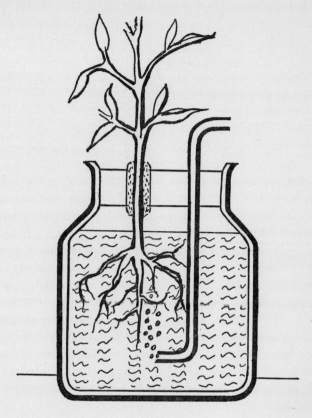

Water culture

definitively established until much more recently, when purification of nutrient substances and refinements of technique made it possible to demonstrate the effect of excluding the trace elements from nutrient solutions.

It is of some importance to distinguish the nutrient cations from the nutrient anions; for when molecules in solution split into their constituent ions, there are equal numbers of positive and negative ions. Now if plants take up more anions than cations, the solution turns alkaline. If they take up more cations than anions, the solution turns acid. Thus elements of positive sign should be paired together so that absorption of one will not leave an excess of the other. For this reason the best salts to use in nutrient solutions are those which can be combined so as to keep the ionic concentration of the solution constant. The three salts, potassium nitrate, calcium phosphate and magnesium sulphate, for example, could be used.

THE ESSENTIAL ELEMENTS

Nitrogen Nitrogen in its free state is a gas, and makes up the greater part of the earth's atmosphere. But it is also one of the chief constituents of proteins, and is in the nucleus of every living cell. It is, too, a constituent of chlorophyll, the chlorophyll molecule containing four nitrogen atoms and one magnesium atom. Since it is involved in all growth processes, and is also a chlorophyll constituent, stunted growth and a pale green colour are the symptoms of deficiency. It is in fact needed in greater quantity than any other mineral element and is the one most likely to be deficient, and to limit growth. It may constitute 2 per cent or more of the plant's dry matter. Plants growing in soil which is rich in nitrogen develop an abundance of leafy growth, and they need and transpire much water. Much of the nitrogen is taken up in the early stages of growth, so that young plants are rich in nitrogen and protein. At maturity nitrogen is transferred to seeds and fruits.

Plants absorb nitrogen in two main forms: as nitrate, and as ammonium. In nature the nitrogen in a soil comes mainly from humus or organic matter (decayed plant remains). When a plant dies, its remains return to the soil. There they are slowly decomposed by the soil microbes and reduced to the simple forms of nitrogen and other minerals which can be reabsorbed by the roots of new plants. This is the nitrogen 'cycle', in which the same stock of nitrogen is continuously reused – unless man removes the crop and so breaks the cycle. But the main stock of nitrogen is in the air: some 150,000 tons of it over every acre of ground. Peas, beans, clovers and other legumes are able to 'fix' some of this atmospheric nitrogen with the help of bacteria which live in nodules on their roots. Other free-living bacteria in the soil can also fix atmospheric nitrogen. And since these bacteria thrive in

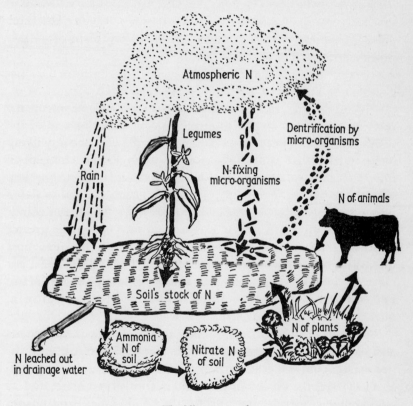

The Nitrogen cycle

soils which contain plenty of organic matter, it is important to build up the organic matter in soils.

This is done by spading crop residues back into the soil, by adding composts and manures, and by green manuring. Green manuring is an old agricultural practice which could be used more in the vegetable garden. Clovers, vetches and lupins are grown and then ploughed under when still green. The nitrogen in their tissues then decomposes in the soil, and the nutrients become available to the new crops.

Soils under old pastures contain much nitrogen. There is less on arable land, especially on light land. Deficiency symptoms are: poor growth, the upper leaves pale green, lower leaves yellow, the lowest leaves yellow and dried. By contrast, when plenty of nitrogen is present, plants make luxurious top growth of a dark green colour.

Phosphorus Phosphorus does not occur free in nature but its compounds are found in many rocks and soils. Natural rock phosphate deposits are mined in North Africa. They contain the remains of small aquatic creatures from evaporated seas.

Like nitrogen, phosphorus is present in the plant cell nucleus, in fats and enzymes, and in the energy-rich compounds which are important in metabolism. Phosphorus is contained in the threads which separate the interior of a plant cell as it divides to form new cells. It is thus essential for the early growth of the plant. Like nitrogen it is plentiful in the growing parts. Later on, phosphorus is transferred to the seeds, and is in fact essential for the growth of seeds. It shortens the growing season and hastens maturity, in this respect acting in the opposite way to nitrogen. For this and other reasons there should be a balance between nitrogen and phosphorus.

Phosphorus is thought to stimulate root growth in particular and indeed, since it is needed for the formation of new cells, it necessarily affects the growth of the whole plant. Phosphorus also improves the quality of fruit and makes it keep better.

If phosphorus is deficient, plants are small and stunted. Their leaves are abnormally dark in colour, often a dull greyish green. There may also be purple or reddish pigments, dead tissues in leaves and flowers, and leaf-fall.

In acid soils phosphorus is converted into unavailable forms. Many of the world's soils are short of phosphorus. When poor acid lands are to be improved, phosphates and lime are usually the first fertilisers to be given.

Potassium Potassium is not found in the free state in nature but it is abundant in combined forms in many soils and rocks. Many clay soils contain about 1 per cent of potash (ie about 20,000lb per acre), but usually only about 100lb or less will be in available form.

Potassium compounds are found in all plant and animal tissues. Although it is not a built-in part of the fabric of plant tissues, it is required in large amounts. It is important in the synthesis of proteins, in photosynthesis, and indeed in much of the internal workings of the plant. It seems also to promote health and vigour. Leaves which are rich in potash do not scorch or wilt easily; the leaf transpires less and can use water more economically.

If nitrogen fertilisers are not balanced by adequate potash, top growth becomes soft, thin-celled, subject to attack by pests, easily damaged by frost, and plants are readily blown over by the wind. So when nitrogen and phosphorus fertilisers are given, the resulting growth often needs to be balanced by increased potash.

There are reserves of potash in clay soil. But sandy soils are often deficient. Root crops, such as potatoes, need much potash. In potatoes, abnormally dark green foliage is one of the first deficiency symptoms. Then the older leaves become yellow, the tips and edges of the older leaves turn brown, and gradually the whole leaf becomes affected. In many other plants also the signs are yellowing at the tips and margins of the older (bottom) leaves, developing into areas of dead tissue at the tip and around the edge of the leaf.

Seedlings need plenty of potash. One of the virtues of well-made farmyard manure is that it can release potash to young plants in quantity without risk of damage.

Calcium Calcium, which is contained in lime and limestone, is used more to improve soil conditions than to supply plant food. But apart from its role as a sweetener of acid soils, calcium is needed in fairly large amounts by many plants, especially the cabbage family, beans and other legumes, carrots, tomatoes and apples. Even potatoes have been known to fail in very acid soils for lack of calcium. Calcium is a constituent of cell walls and has many other functions. There is little removal of calcium from the older parts of the plant to the developing buds and shoots, that is, it is not readily redistributed in the tissues. Therefore the

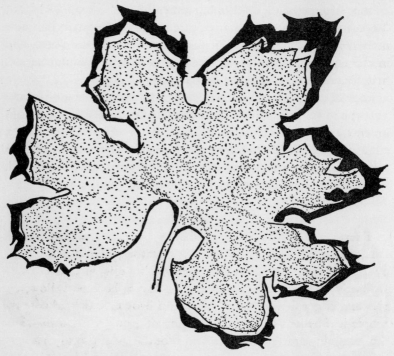

Potassium deficiency in a hop leaf – marginal scorching

symptoms of deficiency occur in the growing points, buds and young leaves and fruits. In tomato plants, for example, upper leaves will yellow while the lower leaves stay green. Some plants such as beet and cauliflower show a 'hooking' backward of the leaf tip, due to uneven growth of the new leaf. The roots of plants are more sensitive to lack of calcium than the parts above ground, the roots being short, much branched, stubby and bulbous. Potato tubers are sensitive indicators of calcium deficiency, being small, malformed and having many 'satellite' tubers.

Calcium is washed out of soils as calcium bicarbonate and sulphate, especially from light soils in areas of heavy rainfall. Some fertilisers such as sulphate of ammonia also displace calcium in the soil, the calcium being lost in drainage water. Because of such losses, liming is used in agriculture on a large scale, many millions of tons of lime being distributed annually.

Magnesium Magnesium is a constituent of chlorophyll. It is also involved in the movement of phosphates within the plant, and in the enzymes. During the ripening of seeds, phosphorus and magnesium move together into the seed.

Lack of magnesium is widespread. The symptoms are distinctive: the lower leaves are usually affected first. They develop light green mottling or chlorosis between the veins and around the edge of the leaf. The affected areas quickly turn brown or pale yellow, and the leaves may die. In addition to the mottling, in some plants the leaf margins become tinted red or orange.

Magnesium deficiency in sweet cherry and vine leaves. Light areas green, dark areas red

Magnesium deficiency occurs mostly on light soils which have been intensely cropped, on acid soils, and in soils which contain much potash. In these last, potash is taken up in preference to magnesium. Magnesium deficiency is perhaps best known in apples and in tomatoes. Lack of magnesium is possibly a greater problem in livestock rearing than in gardening. Grass tetany or 'staggers' affects animals in the spring flush of grass, when the grass contains a high level of nitrogen and potassium and little magnesium or calcium.

Sulphur Sulphur is a constituent of many proteins and of plant hormones, and is also connected with the formation of chlorophyll. Cabbages and onions take up more of it than most plants.

In industrial areas adequate sulphur is brought in by rainfall. Soils also receive sulphur in superphosphate and other fertilisers. But as air pollution is reduced and superphosphate replaced by other phosphate fertilisers, deficiencies of sulphur may arise. Yellowing of new growth may be a sign of lack of sulphur.

Iron Iron acts as a catalyst in photosynthesis, and is also involved in other enzymes. The amounts required are relatively small, and there is plenty of iron in most soils. But even red soils, which contain much iron, do not always provide sufficient, the iron being in unavailable form. Fruit-trees on some chalk soils are frequently affected.

Iron chlorosis may appear quite suddenly in soils which have been over-limed. There is yellowing of the young leaves, the veins often remaining green – iron cannot be moved from one part of the plant to another. The leaves do not die at once, but may turn yellow or near white and stay on the end of a shoot whose older leaves are green.

Iron deficiency also occurs in soils which contain other heavy metals in quantity, such as copper, zinc or manganese. Iron chelates are now available in which the iron is held in the soil in such a way that it cannot be readily 'fixed'.

Manganese Manganese is a constituent of plant enzymes, and is thought to be involved in the leaf chloroplasts and in the process of respiration. In deficiency the older leaves become paler and contain dead spots. The areas around the leaf veins stay dark green but the tissue between the veins fades and the leaves may die and fall. Of all the minor nutrients manganese is the most likely to be deficient in British soils.

Manganese deficiency is the cause of 'marsh spot' (death of the seed leaves within the seed) in peas and broad beans. Potatoes also are often affected. Black spots occur close to the veins of young leaflets, and are followed by chlorotic mottling. In French beans also, dead spots along the veins precede yellow-green mottling of young leaves, leading to bleaching of the entire leaf.

The amount of manganese taken up by the plant varies with the amount available in the soil. On acid soils, plants may contain 1,000 parts per million of manganese, on chalk soils only 10ppm or less. Above pH6·5, manganese becomes unavailable in the soil.

Since manganese can be taken up in large amounts, an excess of the element can also be a problem on acid soils. Brassicas, swedes and beans are susceptible, showing leaf mottling and perforated interveinal areas. Excess uptake will of course not occur on a well-limed soil.

Manganese is also important in animal nutrition. Pigs and poultry which are fed rations lacking in manganese may suffer from crooked legs and enlarged joints.

Copper Copper is required in very small amounts, but is nevertheless necessary in enzyme systems, being found in the chloroplasts of the leaves. Only about 1ppm has to be present in the soil, but if this is lacking plants will suffer.

The symptoms of deficiency are dying back of the growing points, and deformed growth. But often there are no obvious deficiency symptoms. Root crops which benefit from a dressing of copper sulphate seldom show definite symptoms of deficiency, but nevertheless benefit from the dressing. If a deficiency is present, an experimental spraying with Bordeaux mixture or a weak solution of copper sulphate (0·05 per cent $CuSO_4$) would quickly show a response.

Cereal crops are sensitive, and are often affected on reclaimed fens and peat soils. Fruit-trees on sandy soils also suffer; and copper deficiency is widespread in upland districts of Wales, where it results in the disease known as 'swayback' in lambs (a disease of the central nervous system).

Zinc Zinc is necessary to the plant on account of its role, in enzymes, and in cell division and the formation of new cells. A deficiency results in poor growth, small rosetted leaves, and the yellowing of the lower leaves at the tips and edges.

In Florida it is an important cause of failure in citrus trees growing in heavy soils. And in Australia oranges and vines are improved by spraying with zinc sulphate (0·2 per cent). In Britain apple trees on sandy acid soils can be affected.

Molybdenum Molybdenum is required in amounts of less than 1ppm. It acts as a catalyst in the reduction of nitrogen to ammonia by the bacteria of legumes. For other plants also, molybdenum is needed to reduce nitrates to ammonia. The need for it was first discovered in Australia where large areas of sandy soils would not grow clovers without molybdenum.

Deficiency symptoms are leaf chlorosis and the failure of newly formed leaves to develop. 'Whiptail' in cauliflowers results from deficiency: newly formed leaves turn counter clockwise, and the leaf contains nearly all central stem and little leaf.

Sensitive plants include clovers, tomatoes and cauliflowers. Deficiencies are likely to occur on acid soils. Liming the soil increases the available supply of molybdenum.

Some pastures – 'teart' pastures – are so high in molybdenum that they are toxic to grazing animals.

Boron Boron affects the uptake and use of calcium, and the transport of sugars, and has many other functions in the plant. Boron deficiency is widespread, most of the boron in soils being unavailable to plants. Deficiency symptoms include black areas inside cabbage stalks, the browning of the curd of cauliflowers, cracked stems in celery, brown spot inside turnips and beets (heart-rot of sugar beet) and corky core in apples. Brassicas and root crops take up much boron, and may thus induce deficiencies in subsequent crops.

Over-liming can induce a deficiency. Boron is readily leached from soils, and deficiencies are therefore likely on sands and

Page 85   (*Above*) Leafmould compost bays; (*below*) the wasteful practice of
burning organic materials in garden bonfires

Page 86 Severe potassium deficiency in pear leaves. Note marginal chlorosis and necrosis

gravels in districts of high rainfall, particularly if organic manures are not used.

Sodium Sodium is not essential for all plant growth – indeed an excess of salt is a problem on millions of acres throughout the world, especially where land has been reclaimed from the sea. But there are some plants which like salt and others which can use it instead of potash, if potash is in short supply, and a few for which it is essential. It is of particular value to plants which are native to seashores.

Some plants benefit from sodium when potash is deficient; others appear to need it for fullest growth even when potash is abundant:

Plants which benefit from sodium when potash is deficient		*Plants which benefit from sodium in addition to adequate potash*	
Slight benefit	*Some benefit*	*Some benefit*	*Large benefit*
Lettuce	Asparagus	Cabbage	Celery
Onion	Carrot	Kale	Table beet
Potato	Tomato	Mustard	Turnip
Spinach	Barley and cereals	Radish	Mangold
			Sugar beet

Sodium is of course most plentiful in the form of common salt (sodium chloride). But this is not the best form of sodium for garden use. Salt makes clay ground sticky, and the chloride fraction is bad for the quality of such crops as potatoes or beet. So it is better to apply sodium in the form of a fertiliser such as nitrate of soda or potash salts (kainite). For celery or beet, potash salts will be a better fertiliser than potassium chloride (muriate of potash) or sulphate of potash.

Chlorine Chlorine is necessary to plants but there is no record of its ever being deficient, since sufficient is brought in the rain, especially in coastal areas, and a good deal is added to the soil in the form of salt which has been fed to animals. A good supply of chlorine increases the water uptake of plants. Crops which receive chloride of potash usually give a larger yield than those fertilised with sulphate of potash. Plants will take up much chloride if it is available, and this may reduce the uptake of other anions –

F

nitrate, phosphate and sulphates. This leads to poor quality and excess moisture content. Potatoes are less mealy and beets contain less sugar: on such crops, therefore, sulphate of potash is preferred to the chloride.

Cobalt Cobalt is not essential to plants, but it is needed by the nodule bacteria of legumes. Grazing animals also need cobalt so that the bacteria of the rumen can make vitamin B_{12}. And when the element is lacking as it is in many granite soils, animals, especially young sheep, suffer from 'pine' – that is, from emaciation and poor growth.

Other elements which are taken up by plants but which do not seem to serve any useful purpose include aluminium and silicon. Aluminium is plentiful in many soils. In acid soils it becomes soluble and may be toxic to plants. This is the main reason why lettuce and onions, for instance, will not grow well in acid soils; they are sensitive to aluminium excess. But acid-loving species such as azaleas and hydrangeas seem to benefit from it. Hydrangeas may contain as much as 1 per cent of aluminium. The pink flowers of hydrangeas can be converted to blue by adding aluminium sulphate to the soil. But even plants like hydrangeas may suffer if they are fed too much aluminium.

NUTRIENT BALANCE SHEETS

Mineral nutrients are removed from garden soil in two main ways: first, as a result of harvesting or removing crops and parts of plants; and secondly, as a result of the leaching action of rain which washes minerals into the subsoil and out into the drainage waters. Leaching of nitrate and sulphate anions is the most severe. The cations, potassium, calcium and magnesium, are held against leaching in clay but are leached from other soils. Phosphorus is not leached, but reverts to fixed and insoluble forms, especially in acid soils.

A rough balance sheet which shows the input and output of the six major nutrients can be seen on page 89.

Nitrogen tends to be quickly converted to nitrate in the soil, whatever the form in which it is applied. As nitrate, it is either

	Nitrogen	Phosphorus	Potassium	Calcium	Magnesium	Sulphur
Main sources of loss	Leaching Crop removal	Reversion Crop removal	Some leaching and reversion Crop removal	Leaching Crop removal	Leaching Crop removal	Leaching Crop removal
Other losses	Denitrification Volatilisation of ammonia					
Main sources of gain	Release from organic matter Biological fixation in legumes	Release from organic matter Parent materials	Parent materials (clays)	Parent materials (lime and chalk)	Parent materials (dolomitic limestone)	Rainfall Release from organic matter
Other gains	Rainfall Lightning					
Incidentally supplied in	Farmyard manure Nitrogen fertilisers	Farmyard manure Phosphorus fertilisers	Farmyard manure Potassium fertilisers	Farmyard manure Wood ashes	Farmyard manure Magnesium fertilisers Basic slag	Farmyard manure Super-phosphate Gypsum Sulphate of ammonia

rapidly absorbed by plant roots or just as rapidly leached into the lower soil layers by rain, if there are no plants growing to absorb it. Nitrogen is also lost through denitrification in waterlogged soil, and through volatilisation of ammonia. A little is brought in by rainfall and by lightning.

Very little phosphorus gets into the soil solution. It tends to be precipitated in more or less insoluble forms as calcium phosphate which is sparingly soluble or, in acid soils, as iron and aluminium phosphates which are insoluble. Organic compounds of phosphorus, which have accumulated from plant residues, are a good source of phosphorus in the tropics but are of less importance in temperate climates. Since phosphorus is so little soluble, it cannot move to the root as the more mobile elements do; plant roots have to grow into contact with it. Thus species differences in ability to extract phosphorus depend to a great extent on the depth and proliferation of the root system.

There are large amounts of potassium in many clays and loams. But most of it is not available, being inside soil particles or in insoluble forms. The soil solution contains very little soluble potassium, but the small amounts which are in solution are quickly absorbed by plants. The potassium in solution is then replenished from the exchangeable or 'useful' stock of potassium which is held on clay surfaces and in other forms. This exchangeable or 'useful' potassium is seldom released from the total stock at a rate of more than 0·5–1 per cent per annum. Thus if the total stock is 20,000lb, not more than 100–200lb would be released each year, and in some soils the rate of release would not keep pace with plant needs.

In light sands the total stock of potassium is small. And in wet climates potassium is leached from such soils. The potassium which is supplied as fertiliser is mostly held on the soil colloids, and is therefore not likely to move downwards in clays. But in light sands much applied potassium may be leached out.

From this brief survey of the fate of the three major elements which make up the bulk of general fertilisers, it is apparent that much applied fertiliser is never taken up by plants but is either leached out by rains or fixed in the soil in unavoidable form. In an average soil the actual percentages of applied fertilisers which are used by plants are thought to be, approximately:

	Nitrogen %	Phosphorus %	Potassium %
Used by plant	50	20	50
Leached by rain	50	Nil	25
Fixed in soil	Nil	80	25

And in acid sands under heavy rain, fertiliser uptake would be a good deal less.

A further and more difficult problem is to ensure that nutrients are available to plants at the right time and in the right amounts. The great virtue of farmyard manure is that it releases minerals slowly and continuously at about the rates which young plants require, whereas fertilisers, especially nitrates, act too quickly so that the young plant takes up the nutrient in excess.

Turning to the other major nutrients, the role of calcium as an essential nutrient tends to be overlooked, since calcium is added to soils mainly to make them less acid, not to provide a supply of the element. Calcium is relatively abundant in nature and is likely to be deficient only in districts of high rainfall, on sandstones and light sandy soils. Nevertheless, calcium is continually being leached from the arable soils of humid climates, necessitating massive replacement.

It exists in soil as free calcium carbonate, as a constituent of primary minerals, and in exchangeable form on the surfaces of clay and humus particles. There is no problem of availability. The simple calcium compounds stay available. Calcium carbonate, although itself hardly soluble, is soluble in the carbonated water of the soil, forming calcium bicarbonate. For this reason the arable soils of humid regions tend to become decalcified.

Although the amounts of calcium required by many plants are relatively small, some species are large consumers of the element, notably root crops, including potatoes, legumes, tomatoes, cabbages and most kinds of fruit-tree.

Magnesium is slowly released from the soil, more especially from clays, which often contain around 0·5 per cent of magnesium. Like calcium it is absorbed on the exchange complex, but is also dissolved in carbonated water and leached from the soil. It may therefore become deficient in sandy soils during wet periods.

Magnesium deficiency is often induced by heavy application of potassium fertiliser, especially by chloride of potash. The deficiency frequently occurs in orchards, and in greenhouse soils in which tomatoes are given much potash and abundant water. In the past magnesium was seldom added to fertilisers, but it is now increasingly required on light soils, as farmyard manure is less used. Farmyard manure was often a useful source of magnesium.

Rain brings in some magnesium, especially in industrial areas. Magnesium is also present in fair amounts in some basic slags, if dolomite was used in their manufacture, and most limestones and chalk contain some magnesium. Soils derived from dolomitic limestone contain both calcium and magnesium, and magnesian limestones may contain as much magnesium carbonate as calcium carbonate.

The supply of sulphur is more than adequate in the industrial areas of the temperate zones. The rain brings down as much sulphur as crops require. But in the non-industrial areas of the more arid zones, sulphur deficiencies are widespread: in Australia and New Zealand, in Central Africa, in Central Canada and on the north-west coast of the USA.

Sulphur, as sulphate, is readily leached from surface soils, although subsoil clays often contain large amounts. Soil organic matter is an important reservoir of sulphur, the sulphur in organic compounds being released as sulphate through the action of bacteria, in much the same way as nitrogen is released as nitrate.

Sulphur is often supplied incidentally in such fertilisers as sulphate of ammonia and superphosphate. But now that fertilisers are taking more refined and concentrated forms, this source of supply may diminish.

In summary, a nutrient balance sheet for the soil has to take into account, on the one hand, the inherent ability of the soil to supply nutrients plus the fertilisers and manures applied, plus nutrients released from plant residues, plus nutrients brought in by rain; and on the other side of the balance sheet, the nutrients removed in crops and plants, plus losses by leaching, fixation, volatilisation, etc. At the end of a growing season there will of course always be a residue in the soil and its organic matter.

NUTRIENTS REMOVED BY PLANTS

In nature nutrients are continuously recycled: grazing animals return minerals to the soil in their manure or the plant dies and its remains return to the soil. In the garden this natural cycle is often broken. The obsessional tidiness of many gardeners leads them to sweep up and burn fallen leaves or to consign plant remains to a rubbish heap. Hedges are constantly clipped and lawns cut, and the clippings and lawn mowings are removed or burnt. In flower and vegetable gardens both tops and roots of plants are removed from the soil. A crop of potatoes, for instance, removes large amounts of nutrients from the soil:

	Removed by average crop (per acre) (lb)	Soluble in soil* (average range) (lb)	Total present in soil but not all available (average range) (lb)
Nitrogen	100	20–200	1,000–10,000
Potassium	100	40–200	5,000–50,000
Calcium	40	100–5,000	10,000–100,000
Magnesium	20	100–1,000	2,000–100,000
Phosphorus	20	20–100	1,000–10,0000
Iron	0·5	10–200	2,000–100,000
Manganese	0·5	10–200	100–10,000
Zinc	0·2	2–20	20–500
Boron	0·2	1–5	4–100
Copper	0·1	1–20	2–200
Molybdenum	0·01	0·002–1	0·5–10

* Column 2 gives some idea of the average amounts of each mineral which are soluble (available to the plant), and column 3 the total stock of minerals in average soils, most of which becomes available only very slowly.

It is evident that in some soils there will not be enough nitrogen or phosphorus or potassium to produce a good crop; and further, if soils are cropped for a number of years without manures or fertilisers having been put back, the point is soon reached at which some of the elements will become short.

This hard fact was recognised by the earliest gardeners and agriculturists, who practised a shifting form of cultivation. They would clear and burn off a patch of land and crop it for one or more seasons; then as the soil fertility declined, they would move on and clear a fresh patch. Those who have had the good fortune to make a garden out of old pasture or rich grassland that has not previously been dug up, will know the extraordinary yields that can be obtained from this virgin soil. But unless there is regular replacement of the minerals which crops remove from the soil, fertility soon declines. The way in which farm soils can deteriorate was well understood by past generations of farmers. Arable land had to be kept in 'good heart'. This was done by keeping strictly to rotations. The best known of these was the British four-course Norfolk rotation of roots dressed with manure, barley, clover and wheat, grown in successive years. Since the crops were varied year by year the same kind of demand was not made on the soil reserves annually, and the inclusion of clover in the rotation enabled the nitrogen supply to be renewed. Landlords would usually insist that a rotation should be followed. And they would not allow tenant farmers to sell hay off the farm; the nutrients contained in the hay had to be conserved by feeding them to stock, so that they would be returned to manure the farm soil. Gardeners could well heed these old practices of rotation; and if they remove grass cuttings from their lawns (which is the same as removing hay from a meadow), they should replace the lost nutrients by regular dressings of fertiliser.

If a soil has been well manured for many years, it will have substantial reserves of nutrients. And the residues will have some small effect for perhaps as long as twenty or thirty years afterwards. But in all years after the first the yield will be less than it was originally. In fact yield drops off in a curve which falls very steeply in the first few years, then decreases at a slower rate, until after some twenty years of continuous cropping without manures, yield will be down to perhaps one-eighth of the previous level or, more likely, many crops will fail to grow at all. Such old and exhausted garden soils are by no means uncommon.

CHAPTER 5

FERTILISERS

And a more luscious Earth for them did knead
Which stupified them while it fed.

(Marvell)

A fertile soil can supply the essential nutrients in the amounts and
at the rates which plants require. Plant roots extract nutrients
from three main sources in the soil: from the soil solution, from
the exchangeable ions held on clay and humus and, to a lesser
extent, from some of the more readily decomposed soil particles.
By far the greater part of the soil minerals is not in available
form; for example, iron salts may make up as much as 10 per
cent of the total soil weight yet be almost entirely unavailable.
It is therefore difficult to determine by straight chemical analysis
how much of the soil materials are available to plants. In practice,
weak extractants such as dilute citric acid or very dilute sulphuric
acid, which simulate the extractive power of roots, are used to
estimate the quickly available fraction of each element.

The composition of the soil solution, although of obvious
importance in nutrition, bears little relation to the nutrient
powers of the soil; that is, of the long-term capacity of the soil
to supply nutrients. Some of the most important elements,
especially potassium and phosphorus, occur only in minute
amounts in the solution. But the level of nutrient in the solution
is constantly being renewed from the solid phase of the soil. It
is therefore just as important to know the rate at which the elements
in solution are renewed as to know its composition. The soil

solution is very dilute, containing not more than 0.05-0.08 per cent of solids, even when the soil is dry.

The supply of nitrogen depends on the rate at which micro-organisms decompose plant remains. This in turn depends largely on the temperature and moisture content of the soil. Unlike the other elements, nitrogen is not derived from parent rock.

Phosphorus is present in soils mostly in insoluble forms. In addition, when phosphates are added to the soil they are often rapidly fixed or precipitated in insoluble forms. The total amount

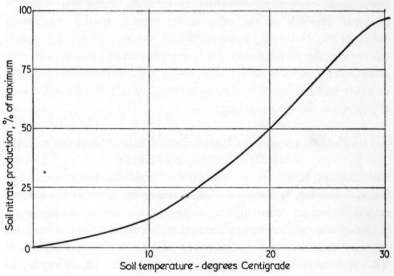

Nitrate production as a function of soil temperature

of phosphorus in the soil solution at any one time is therefore small (1-2ppm) in relation to the need of plants. It is constantly renewed from the solid phase, but often not fast enough to meet the needs of growing plants.

Calcium, magnesium and potassium are adsorbed on clay and humus particles as exchangeable cations. Afterwards, they may pass into the soil solution or may be taken up directly in contact exchange. The cation-exchange capacity of a soil is a measure of the total exchange capacity for the three main cations, for sodium, and also, in acid soils, for hydrogen. The exchange complex is usually dominated by calcium ions and holds relatively few potassium ions. The exchangeable potassium may therefore be readily depleted. In general, clay soils and those high in organic matter have a high exchange capacity, holding the nutrient cations from being leached from the soil. Sandy soils on the other hand have a low capacity and are very likely to be deficient in these elements.

The other major nutrient, sulphur, is present in soils as sulphate and also in organic compounds; in fact, the amount of sulphur in a soil depends on the amount of organic matter contained. Most of the inorganic sulphur which is released from organic matter is in the form of sulphate, in combination with cations such as calcium. In this form it tends to be leached from the soil, but in many areas of the world enough sulphur is brought in in rainfall to meet the needs of plants.

METHODS OF DETERMINING THE AMOUNTS OF FERTILISER NEEDED

Manures and fertilisers are applied first with the object of correcting deficiencies, and then of maintaining fertility. Few soils are naturally fertile. Many old garden soils are impoverished as a result of years of inadequate manuring, the burning or destruction of plant residues, and the leaching of bare soil by winter rains. The best remedial treatment for general nutrient deficiency is farmyard manure, which not only improves physical structure but also supplies elements which are not present in nitrogen, phosphorus and potassium fertilisers. The use of fertilisers needs to be based on careful observation and inquiry. The indiscriminate use of 'general' fertilisers is wasteful and may well do harm.

To express at all accurately the relation of mineral nutrition to the growth of plants, an equation would have to be written which would contain many unknowns. In practice, the possible methods of assessing the need of the soil for manures and fertilisers are:

1   Observation of plants growing in the garden and in the

neighbourhood. The experience of skilled local gardeners is obviously invaluable. In addition, inferences can be made from knowledge of local soil types and soil series. Regional horticultural advisers and soil chemists will have much accumulated knowledge about the soils in their areas, and can give useful general advice – although soils can vary immensely within a small area. Nevertheless, some basic generalisations can usually be made. In Britain, for example, most clays lack phosphorus but have adequate potassium. Sandy soils are more generally deficient and often lack potassium and magnesium. On chalk potassium is very deficient and fruit typically suffers from iron deficiency. Fenland and black organic soils lack copper and manganese. Generalisations can also be made about more limited areas. For example, the clay-with-flints overlying the Upper Chalk is deficient in lime and phosphorus. All such background knowledge is at least suggestive.

2   Experimental strips or plots may be set up in the garden. In the simplest arrangement, half a row of plants is treated with a fertiliser which is omitted on the other half of the row, and the difference between the two halves is visually observed or more systematically assessed by some measure of the yield.

3   Chemical analysis of soil and plant, which suggests itself most readily as a scientific approach, is in fact beset with many difficulties. The results of soil chemical analysis can be translated into fertiliser recommendation only by those who have much knowledge of local soils. 'Quick' tests marketed for amateur use are unreliable. Even the soil testing which is carried out by fully equipped laboratories is not always valid. As plants grow, they need a continuously adequate supply of mineral nutrients. The supply depends on (a) the concentration or intensity of the nutrients, (b) the capacity of the soil to maintain the necessary concentration and (c) the rate at which nutrients are released or renewed as they are removed by plants. Intensity is measured as the concentration of the element in the soil solution. Capacity is measured by the amount of exchangeable nutrient which can come into the soil solution. The renewal rate is measured by the

rate of transfer from solid to solution. But most soil tests measure
only the intensity factor.

Of the major nutrients, calcium is the only element which pre-
sents no problems in soil analysis. The lack of a useful soil test for
nitrogen is especially unfortunate.

Plant analysis offers a more direct measure of nutrient availability. Tissue testing is a quick method of assessing the concentration of nutrients in the cell sap. A tomato plant, for example,
can be tested by splitting the stalk, inserting filter paper, and
pressing the stalk against it, so as to obtain a sample of sap. The
sap is then tested for the major nutrients, using several different
reagents.

4 Standard, rule-of-thumb recommendations may be followed.
Since it is not easy to obtain any precise information about either
the soil's power to supply nutrients or about the plants' needs, the
easiest course is to fall back on standard recommendations. These
are dealt with at length in Chapter 10. These recommendations
are usually based on the assumption that the nutrient supplying
power of the soil is zero, that the fertilisers applied will all be
taken up in the growing season, and that the residue in the soil
is zero. This is of course by no means the case. If applied annually,
both phosphorus and potassium tend to accumulate in soils. So,
once deficiencies have been set right, heavy annual applications
of phosphorus and potassium may not be necessary. In commercial
practice, large annual doses are given in order to effect maximum
yield, fertiliser costs being a small part of the total cost of production. Most gardeners will not wish to spoliate their soil in quest
of higher yields; for the consequences of heavy annual dressings
of nitrogen, phosphorus and potassium fertiliser may be magnesium and other deficiencies, high salt concentration and the
accumulation of the undesirable 'ballast' of fertiliser in the soil.
Over-fertilisation with inorganic fertilisers reduces the uptake of
water, causes foliage to wilt and leaf margins to become scorched.
There is often a white accumulation of salts on the surface of the
soil – frequently seen on the soil of pot plants. In commercial
practice, the salt content of glasshouse soils is estimated by

measuring the electrical conductivity of the soil. The effects of salinity on growth are negligible when the conductivity (expressed in mm per cm) is less than 2 (equivalent to a resistance of $1/0.002 = 5000$ ohms). When the salt index rises much above this figure, containers or beds should be flooded periodically with water to leach away the accumulated salts.

NITROGEN FERTILISERS

Nitrogen fertilisers are in the form of nitrate, ammonium or urea. They are all water-soluble. Nitrate is the swiftest acting and the most readily lost. But ammonium is quickly converted into nitrate by soil microbes at temperatures above $12°$ C. Urea is converted to ammonia and then to nitrate.

Commonly available forms of nitrogen fertiliser include:

	Chemical formula	Relative acidity/ alkalinity	%N	
Sulphate of ammonia	$(NH_4)_2SO_4$	−110	21	Makes the soil acid. Can be applied dissolved in water
Nitrochalk	NH_4NO_3 $CaCO_3$	+60	15·5	Mixture of ammonium nitrate and chalk. Contains both ammonia and nitrate
Urea	$CO(NH_2)_2$	−80	45	Highly concentrated
Nitrate of soda (Chilean nitrate)	$NaNO_3$	+29	15·5	Bad effects on soil structure
Calcium nitrate (nitrate of lime)	$Ca(NO_3)_2$	+20	15·5	Highly deliquescent

The approximate nutrient percentages in each fertiliser can be obtained from the molecular weights. The molecular weight of sulphate of ammonia, for example, is $(14 + 4)2 + 32 + 16 \times 4 = 132$. The nitrogen component is $28/132 \times 100 = 21$ per cent.

Sulphate of ammonia In many countries sulphate of ammonia is still the most common and the most readily available nitrogen fertiliser. It is not readily leached from the soil, the ammonium being held on the clay-humus complex. There the ammonium ion usually displaces calcium, and the soluble sulphate which results is then readily leached. (In sandy soils without much clay or humus it will of course not be held, and will be lost more quickly.) Since it displaces calcium, and is itself replaced by hydrogen ions on nitrification, it makes the soil more acid; 100lb of sulphate of ammonia needs 110lb of limestone to neutralise its acid effect. While its acidifying property may be of advantage for acid-loving plants and in calcareous soils, it is, in this respect, usually injurious in the garden.

The ammonium in sulphate of ammonia can be absorbed directly by plants, but it does not act quite as quickly as nitrate. It is cheap, handles and stores better than nitrate and urea, but will probably in time be replaced by more concentrated fertilisers.

Nitrochalk In order to overcome acidifying effects, nitrochalk also contains lime. Nitrochalk contains both ammonia and nitrate in the form of ammonium nitrate; and since these two forms of nitrogen will be released at different rates, it should have effect over a longer period than either ammonia or nitrate separately.

Urea Urea is highly concentrated (45 per cent nitrogen) and cheap, but it stores badly. In the soil it is converted to ammonium carbonate. Free ammonia is liberated and may be lost unless the urea is well buried in the soil. Urea, like other ammonium salts, will damage germinating seeds and should not be placed near the seed row. Its main advantage apart from cheapness is that it is less subject to leaching loss than the other forms of nitrogen. It is a common constituent of compound fertilisers.

Nitrate of soda Chilean deposits of nitrate of soda provided the first artificial fertilisers. Synthetic sodium nitrate is now manufactured. Plants respond more quickly to nitrates than to other forms of nitrogen. Nitrate of soda has long been used as a top or side dressing on growing crops, the effect often being visible within two or three days. The sodium of nitrate of soda is of value to plants such as beets and celery, which respond to salt.

Both sodium and calcium nitrate absorb moisture and are difficult to handle, and to store, unless kept in airtight polythene bags.

Page 103 Effect of soil acidity on young apple trees. Note die-back of shoots due to high manganese content in bark causing necrosis and subsequent death of shoots, bark and main stem

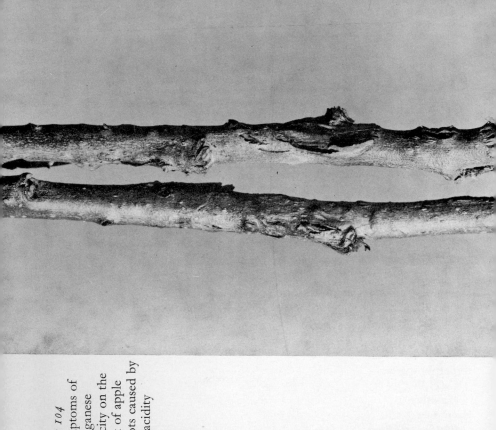

Symptoms of
manganese
toxicity on the
bark of apple
shoots caused by
soil acidity

PHOSPHORUS FERTILISERS

In most countries the main phosphorus fertiliser is still super-phosphate. This is the oldest artificial fertiliser, first patented in 1842. It is made by treating rock phosphates with sulphuric acid which converts them into more soluble compounds. In addition, calcium sulphate (gypsum) is formed, which has some fertilising value in its own right. Superphosphate usually contains about 18 per cent of available phosphoric acid. It also contains more trace elements, especially copper and zinc, than most other ferti-lisers. Higher grades, double and treble superphosphate, are also obtainable.

The main phosphorus fertilisers are:

	Available P_2O_5 %	Total lime CaO %	Total magnesium MgO %	Total sulphate %
Superphosphate $Ca(H_2PO_4)_2$ (mostly)	14–20	24–30	0·5	25–32
Basic slag $(CaO)_5 . P_2O_5$ SiO_2	5–15	45	2·5	0·5
Ground rock phosphate	18	32	18	Nil
Bone-meal $Ca_3(PO_4)_2$	20–5	30	1	0·5

Basic slag is a by-product of the steel industry. Its phosphorus is insoluble in water but soluble in water containing carbon dioxide. It is useful on acid soils, especially on grass. Ground rock phosphate is likewise mainly of use on acid soils in districts of high rainfall. Both supply useful amounts of magnesium and some of the trace elements.

In the table, 'Available' is something of a misnomer. The phosphate in superphosphate is soluble in water, but in the soil it is fairly quickly precipitated in the top few inches of soil, and in acid soils it is fixed in unavailable iron and aluminium

G

compounds. Rock phosphates and bone-meal on the other hand are not water-soluble, and in wet climates on acid soils they have more chance of coming into solution and are less likely to be fixed, since their phosphorus is combined with calcium and does not react with iron and aluminium.

Bone-meal tends to be preferred by gardeners to the inorganic forms of phosphorus. Its phosphorus is released slowly in the soil, and it is therefore thought to be of especial value when planting trees, shrubs or other perennials which need a lasting supply of phosphorus. There is no evidence, however, that it is better than superphosphate, except perhaps in acid soils in which superphosphate rapidly becomes fixed.

POTASSIUM FERTILISERS

The two main potassium fertilisers are potassium chloride and potassium sulphate. Potassium salts are obtained mostly from brine and from soluble minerals mined from underground deposits.

	Water-soluble potash K_2O %	Lime	Magnesia	Sulphate
Potassium chloride KCl (muriate of potash)	48–60	Nil–2	Nil–2	Nil–7
Potassium sulphate (sulphate of potash) K_2SO_4	48–52	Nil–2	Nil–2	40–8
Wood ashes K_2CO_3	4–10	30–40		

The sulphate, although more expensive, is generally to be preferred in the garden. The chloride anions of potassium chloride are very soluble and may raise the salt concentration of the soil solution to a level which damages young plants. The mobile chloride anions may also antagonise uptake of phosphates. They may also cause marginal leaf scorch in some plants. The sulphate form is more suitable for soft fruits and for tomatoes and potatoes. It is also much easier to store than the chloride form.

Fresh wood ashes contain useful amounts of potash and lime, together with lesser quantities of other nutrients.

MAGNESIUM FERTILISERS

Magnesium fertilisers are most likely to be needed by fruit-trees and by vegetables growing in sandy soils. Magnesium is also needed in peat-based composts and peat seed blocks.

The preferred source on acid soils will usually be magnesian limestone, which may contain as much as 50 per cent of magnesium carbonate. Ordinary limestones may also contain useful amounts of magnesium.

Otherwise the most commonly used magnesium fertilisers are:

	Magnesium %
Epsom salts ($MgSO_4 . 7H_2O$)	9·6
Kieserite ($MgSO_4 . H_2O$)	18·3
Kainite or potash salts	3–4
Basic slag	4–5

Farmyard manure also contains about 0·1 per cent magnesium.

Where an actual deficiency of magnesium exists, it is more rapidly corrected by foliar sprayings with Epsom salts or kieserite than by soil applications.

ORGANIC FERTILISERS: ANALYSIS

Many gardeners are prepared to pay high prices for such organic fertilisers as dried blood, bone-meal and hoof- and horn-meal, in the belief that they possess virtues not found in inorganic fertilisers. Organic fertilisers are very variable in composition, but average figures yielded by chemical analysis are:

	Nitrogen %	Phosphorus %	Potassium %	Calcium %	Magnesium %
Dried blood	12	1	1	0·2	Nil
Hoof and horn	14	1	Nil	1·8	Nil
Animal tankage	7	4	0·4	11	0·3
Fish manure	9	3	Nil	6	0·3
Wool waste (shoddy)	3	0·2	2	Nil	Nil
Bone-meal	4	10	Nil	22	0·6
Steamed bone-flour	2·5	11	Nil	24	0·3
Dried seaweed	1·5	0·2	4	2	0·6
Peat moss	2	Nil	Nil	0·7	0·3
Wood ashes	Nil	1	4	23	2
Sewage sludge	1	0·3	Nil	2	0·3

Most organic fertilisers are used because they are good sources of nitrogen. Bone-meal and bone-flour are good sources of phosphorus. But few organics are complete fertilisers as farmyard manure is, for they contain little or no potash.

THE MERITS OF ORGANIC FERTILISERS

Experimental work has shown that organic sources of nitrogen such as blood-meal, hoof-meal and fish-meal produce no greater yields of vegetables than equivalent amounts of sulphate of ammonia. Whether they yield better quality of produce than commercial fertilisers would also seem open to doubt as they contain no potash. Neither do they improve soil structure.

One advantage usually claimed for them is that they are 'foolproof'; that is, they can be applied in large amounts without damaging or 'burning' crops. Their nitrogen is supposedly released at a slow rate, and presumably is less likely to be washed out of a soil than the nitrates in artificials. Hoof- and horn-meal, for example, is supposed to act slowly, in contrast to dried blood, which acts quickly. But there is doubt about this, and apparently the finer grades form inorganic nitrogen quickly.

Bone-meal as a source of phosphorus continues to be highly prized by gardeners. Bone-meal has some advantages over superphosphate, but only on wet and acid soils. The tricalcium phosphate in bone-meal is only slowly soluble in the soil, but it does not become fixed in acid soils, as superphosphate does. Although the water-soluble phosphate of superphosphate is more available than the insoluble phosphate of bone-meal, in acid soils below pH5·5 superphosphate, especially if it is in powdered form, is quickly fixed in the soil. Therefore, bone-meal may be better in these soils. But there is some doubt about this: some authorities claim that superphosphate, although rapidly fixed, is not so firmly fixed – at least for some months – that it cannot be used by growing plants.

The advantages which organic nitrogen fertilisers have over inorganics are that they may contain more trace elements, have a rate of release more in keeping with plant requirements, and be less likely to damage young plants or to leave high residual concentrations of salts in the soil.

Wood ashes can be a fair source of phosphate, potash and lime and are prized by gardeners for applying to fruit-bushes.

Sewage sludges provide nitrogen and phosphorus but their potash is less available than the potash in farmyard manure. They also sometimes contain such high amounts of metal, like copper and zinc, that they are actually toxic to plants. Experimental work has shown sludge to be generally much inferior to farmyard manure, although it is effective on cabbages, since it supplies the nitrogen they require.

GRADES OF FERTILISER

In order to supply a total of, say, 10lb of nitrogen, it is easy to calculate that 50lb of sulphate of ammonia (20 per cent nitrogen) would be required, or 62lb of nitrate of soda (16 per cent nitrogen), or 83lb of dried blood (12 per cent nitrogen).

The calculation of the amounts of phosphorus and potassium in fertilisers is a little more complicated. It was, and often still is, the custom to express amounts of phosphorus in terms of phosphoric acid (P_2O_5) rather than in terms of the element P; and to express amounts of potash as K_2O rather than in terms of the element K. There is no good reason for the older usage and modern practice is to specify fertiliser amounts in terms of the elements. Conversion to the older form is in fact simple:

$$2\tfrac{1}{3} \times P = P_2O_5$$
$$1\tfrac{1}{5} \times K = K_2O$$

Compound or ready-mixed fertilisers are described by grades. These grades indicate the percentage content of nitrogen (N), phosphoric acid (P_2O_5) and water-soluble potash (K_2O). A 5–10–5 fertiliser contains 5 per cent nitrogen, 10 per cent available phosphoric acid and 5 per cent soluble potash. The nutrient ratio is 1:2:1. A 10–20–10 grade would similarly have a 1:2:1 ratio but would contain 40 per cent total nutrients as against 20 per cent of the 5–10–5 grade. If only two major nutrients are included, the grade would be given as eg 0–14–14, containing no nitrogen but 14 per cent each of phosphoric acid and potash.

The nutrient content of fertilisers will eventually be expressed in terms of the elements, N, P and K. Then an 8–16–16 fertiliser (old style) will become approximately 8–7–13 (new style).

In recent years more concentrated compounds have begun to replace the older grades such as 5–10–10. A more concentrated fertiliser is clearly less bulky and easier to store and to spread. But it has some disadvantages. It is more likely to damage young seedlings, and it is less likely to contain small quantities of other useful nutrient elements.

STRAIGHT VERSUS COMPOUND FERTILISERS

Compound fertilisers are time-saving and easy to apply, especially if they are in granulated form. But many compounds deteriorate in storage since the commonly used forms of nitrogen and potash are hygroscopic. Compounds therefore often become sticky or cemented. Unless many fertiliser grades are stocked, the NPK ratio cannot be adjusted to the needs of individual plants. Moreover, the actual fertiliser ingredients of compounds are not generally stated, only the percentages of each element. The user therefore does not know whether the nitrogen component is, say, sulphate of ammonia (which may be useful to brassicas, as containing sulphur) or some other form of nitrogen; nor whether the potassium component is the chloride form – which is undesirable for many culinary plants – or the sulphate form. Many proprietary fertilisers contain organic nitrogen such as hoof and horn, or organic phosphorus such as bone-meal, in the hope that these nutrients will be gradually released. Such fertilisers are expensive in relation to the more common 'straight' fertilisers.

Straight fertilisers are more adaptable to the needs of particular plants. Nitrogen can be given in several applications so that it is not leached from the soil. Phosphorus can be banded in the soil where seedling roots can use it for their early growth. And potassium may also be given in several dressings, to avoid 'luxury consumption' and magnesium antagonism. Straight fertilisers can be applied in much more controlled and flexible fashion than compounds, and will normally be preferred by those who wish to give detailed attention to the nutrition of their plants.

MIXING OF FERTILISERS

When NPK fertilisers are mixed, the constituents must be compatible. Some ingredients cannot be mixed together without loss; others can be mixed if they are applied at once to the soil; while others can be mixed and stored.

Firstly, lime and substances containing lime should not be mixed with ammonium compounds, otherwise the volatile alkali ammonia is expelled. This means that lime, basic slag or nitrochalk should not be mixed with sulphate of ammonia, for example. For the same reason lime should not be mixed with farmyard manure.

Secondly, superphosphate should not be mixed with fertilisers containing nitrates and chlorides. Otherwise volatile substances will be expelled. This means that nitrate of soda, nitrochalk and chloride of potash should not be mixed with superphosphate, although it is possible to do so if the mixture is to be applied to the soil at once.

A storable mixture can be compounded from sulphate of ammonia, superphosphate and sulphate of potash.

INJURY TO PLANTS BY FERTILISERS

Young plants and germinating seedlings are often killed or injured by fertilisers. And leaves are easily scorched by the dust from top-dressings of nitrogen. In fact, the careless or uninformed use of fertilisers may produce effects which partially justify the 'organic' gardeners' distrust of them.

Injury from fertilisers arises in three main ways. Firstly, a high salt concentration, especially of nitrates and chlorides, interferes with the uptake of water. Secondly, some fertiliser ingredients are directly damaging to plant tissues, especially some nitrogen fertilisers. Thirdly, ammonium nitrogen, if regularly applied without the use of lime, causes soil acidity and reduces the supply of the metallic cations, potassium, magnesium and calcium.

A high salt concentration in the soil results in an increase in its osmotic pressure, that is in the tenacity with which the solution is held in the soil. If the solutes of the soil solution are present as ions, particularly if they are electrolytes of the sodium chloride or potassium chloride type, this effect is increased. Chloride and nitrate anions tend to be concentrated in the soil solution, since they are not held on the soil colloids. Old greenhouse soils and nursery beds, which in the past have received much nitrate or chloride of potash, tend to have excessive salt accumulations and are said to be 'sick'. They often contain large amounts of calcium sulphate which are the residues of superphosphate and sulphate of ammonia. Such residues may interfere with the normal uptake of potassium and other minerals. Much the same conditions are met in naturally saline soils.

Nitrogen fertilisers damage germinating seeds directly, especially the larger seeds such as beans and peas. And ammonium fertilisers and urea may produce, in the presence of lime, gas which is toxic to germinating seedlings. Of commonly used fertilisers, urea, sodium nitrate, chloride of potash and sulphate of ammonia all have high salt indices, and may well have adverse effects on germination. Sulphate of potash is less damaging, and super-phosphate least.

It is unfortunate, then, that while young plants need to take up much of their nitrogen, phosphorus and potassium in the early stages of growth, high concentrations of NPK fertilisers are lethal when placed near the germinating seeds. It is probable that many gardeners look in vain for the emergence of seedlings, having dressed the seed rows with sulphate of ammonia or one of the more concentrated nitrogen fertilisers.

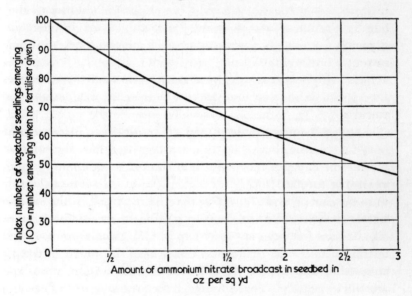

Damage to germinating seeds by inorganic nitrogen

Damage can be avoided by banding fertilisers in the soil some distance from the seed, by keeping seed beds moist, and by avoiding the use of inorganic nitrogen and chloride of potash in seed beds and seed composts. The well-tried John Innes composts, for example, include only superphosphate and lime in seed composts, and an organic source of nitrogen, hoof and horn, together with superphosphate and sulphate of potash, in potting composts.

Some animal manures, especially pig and poultry manures, will also scorch and damage young plants if they are applied fresh. When rotted or composted, they lose much of their quick-acting ammonia and may then be more safely applied.

PLACEMENT OF FERTILISERS

In placing fertiliser in the soil some account must be taken of the feeding zone of the plant roots, and of the movement of soil minerals to the root. Roots grow so as to be in direct contact with some small percentage of fertiliser particles. Other particles are dissolved in the soil solution, which is then carried to the roots as a result of transpiration. But the soil solution contains only minute quantities of phosphorus and potassium, which reach the root more slowly through diffusion.

Uptake of phosphorus is important in early growth, yet phosphate fertilisers tend to become rapidly fixed in soils, especially in acid soils. The problem then is to provide the young plant with a supply of phosphorus and other nutrients placed close enough to be readily reached by the young root, but not so close that it will damage the plant. The accepted solution of this problem is to place a band of superphosphate in the seed bed, 2in to the side of, and 2in below, the seed. By banding the superphosphate rather than broadcasting it, it is less in contact with the soil, and therefore does not react into insoluble compounds. If the superphosphate is in granulated rather than in powdered form, the reaction will be less. When placed in this position, the fertiliser will be readily reached by the lateral roots of most species. But tap-rooting species and those with restricted root systems, such as french beans or onions, may more easily reach the band of fertiliser if it is placed about 3in directly underneath the seed.

Plants which have large seeds can easily reach fertiliser bands some distance from the seed, since their roots grow down into the soil about 6in within ten days of germination. But very small seeds may not be able to make much root growth in a poor soil, and their food reserves may be exhausted before the band of fertiliser can be tapped. If small-seeded crops are to be grown on a soil which is naturally thin and poor, some organic manure needs to be put close to the seed. The Chinese put manure directly along the seed row.

Ammonium nitrogen, such as sulphate of ammonia, physically mixed in with the superphosphate in the band, increases the uptake of superphosphate and brings about a thicker and more robust growth of root. It is not clear whether this effect is chemical or biological or both, but it does not obtain if the nitrogen is spatially separated from the phosphate; it has to be mixed with it. Since the nitrogen has to be in cationic form, NH_4^+, whereas the phosphate is in anionic form, PO_4^-, it is possible that the entry of the phosphate ions into the root may be facilitated by the presence of ions of opposite charge.

Once past the seedling stage, when plants have developed an extensive root system, the placement of fertiliser becomes less critical and an ordinary broadcast application is usually as effective as any other. But, since many plants quickly send down their roots to considerable depths in the soil, surface applications of phosphorus and potassium should be avoided. Phosphorus and potassium fertilisers need to be dug into the soil, since they move very little; if cast on the surface they are likely to stay there. Nitrogen fertilisers on the other hand are washed downwards in the soil and are unlikely not to be absorbed by plant roots, except in very dry weather. Since phosphorus and potassium fertilisers tend to remain in the surface soil, it may be difficult to place them at a sufficient depth for the roots of trees and other perennials. Therefore, when young trees are planted, these fertilisers should be placed with the deeper soil at the bottom of the planting hole. After planting, fruit-trees can be given the potassium which they need in large amounts by digging holes some 2ft deep and placing fertilisers and manures at depth. Or deep furrows may be drawn and the fertiliser put in deeply, if damage to roots can be avoided.

Much the same considerations apply to the fertilisation of transplants. Much of their root system and root hairs will have been torn away, and they are therefore in poor case to take up water and nutrients. A nutrient or 'starter' solution round the roots speeds root regeneration and further growth. In such starter solutions the main response is from phosphorus. The solution should be very dilute, about ¾oz of superphosphate in 2gal of water, and should not include nitrates or chlorides which might bring about a high salt concentration in the soil.

TIMING OF FERTILISER APPLICATIONS

Plants which have a short growing season need ample nutrients right from the start. The uptake of minerals has to come early in the life of the plant.

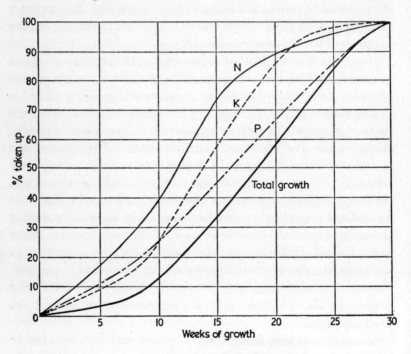

Growth of a cereal plant

After ten weeks the plant has made less than 10 per cent of its total growth, but it has already taken up nearly 40 per cent of its total nitrogen and about 20 per cent of its phosphorus and potassium. When it is half grown it has taken up nearly all the nitrogen and potassium. So the plant makes its greatest demand for minerals when it is young. It can grow rapidly only when the major nutrients are in good supply from the start.

Ideally, fertilisers should be applied at such times as will afford a continuous supply of nutrients in accordance with the needs of growing plants, and yet will avoid leaching and other losses.

Fertilisers may be applied some months before seeding or planting, just before seeding or planting, or at various stages of growth. Nutrients which are likely to be washed from the soil – primarily nitrogen – should not be applied long in advance of seeding, especially in light soils. Nitrogen fertilisers present the most difficult problems of timing. If a single large application is given, it will either be lost in drainage or be taken up by plants in such excess that either the plant will be damaged or the uptake of other nutrients antagonised. Much work is being done on slow-release nitrogen fertilisers, but to date they have not been successful, since the rate of release is not correlated with the changing needs of the plant. In nature a flush of nitrogen occurs as the soil warms up and the increased microbial activity syn-chronises with the growth of plants. But the release of nitrogen from organic matter, although often supplying enough nutrients for flowers and shrubs, does not keep pace with the intensive demands of vegetables and fruit, or with the high demands of the more luxuriant flowers. Unless unusually large quantities of farmyard manure are available, therefore, these crops need sup-plementary nitrogen early in the course of their growth, and it is usual to give side-dressings of nitrogen at least twice in the growing period.

Normally any side-dressings of nitrogen will be washed from the surface to the root by rain, but in prolonged dry weather the fertiliser may have to be watered in. Ammonium nitrogen, such as sulphate of ammonia, may be held on the surface colloids when the soil temperature is less than 12° C. Above this tem-perature it is rapidly converted to nitrate in the soil. In the early spring the soluble nitrates are more readily available and therefore tend to be preferred for early top-dressings. If further applications of nitrogen are given when soil temperatures are higher, either form of nitrogen is equally available.

ANTAGONISM AND INTERACTION BETWEEN NUTRIENT ELEMENTS

There has to be a balance between cations and anions in the soil solution, and also within the plant root. Now, there is competition between ions of the same charge both on the soil particles and at the root membranes. Further, the monovalent ions such as nitrate NO_3^- and potassium K^+ are more mobile than divalent ions such as calcium Ca^{++}. Of the anions, nitrate, and of the cations, potassium, are absorbed in by far the largest quantities. These facts are of practical importance in deciding on the forms and combinations of fertilisers. For example, nitrogen can be applied either as ammonium or as nitrate. Nitrate will tend to increase the uptake of potassium, whereas ammonium will decrease it. Therefore if much potassium is required, its uptake will be facilitated by nitrate nitrogen rather than by ammonium nitrogen.

Since nitrogen, phosphorus and sulphur are all used in building plant organic compounds, they are required in fairly definite relative proportions: if much nitrogen is taken up, it needs to be balanced by increased uptake of phosphorus and sulphur. The cations, potassium, calcium and magnesium on the other hand are not so important in building organic compounds. They need to be present in the plant in order to balance the anions, but their relative proportions can vary widely without affecting plant growth. Potassium ions tend to be absorbed in large quantities, and to inhibit the uptake of calcium and magnesium. But the ratio of potassium/calcium plus magnesium can vary from 1:1 to 1:5 without growth's being affected, at any rate in non-legumes. (Legumes have a higher requirement of calcium.)

In general a high or excessive supply of nitrogen reduces the uptake of many other minerals, and a high or excessive supply of potassium reduces the uptake of other cations. The following antagonisms have been demonstrated:

Ammonium nitrogen is antagonistic to potassium, calcium, magnesium, copper
Nitrate nitrogen is antagonistic to phosphorus
Potassium is antagonistic to calcium, magnesium, boron
Phosphorus is antagonistic to manganese, zinc, copper
Calcium is antagonistic to potassium, magnesium
Magnesium is antagonistic to potassium, calcium

Sometimes it is possible to make use of these antagonisms to control toxicities. For example, manganese toxicity in greenhouse soils may be controlled by the application of phosphates, but it is reduced more readily by raising the soil pH.

The metallic trace elements tend to be mutually antagonistic. The following antagonisms occur:

Iron	Manganese
Manganese	Iron
Zinc	Iron
Copper	Iron, manganese

There are fewer instances of the uptake of one nutrient facilitating another, but the following such 'synergisms' occur:

Phosphorus →Magnesium, molybdenum
Potassium →Iron, manganese
Magnesium →Phosphorus

In general, the uptake of the constituents of compound fertilisers will be best when ion interactions are not antagonistic.

'ORGANIC' GARDENING AND THE EFFECT OF FERTILISERS ON QUALITY

'Organic' gardening still has its champions, in spite of the fact that the enormous increases in yields in the world's agriculture have been achieved by the use of artificial manures. In 1940 Sir Albert Howard, who had spent a lifetime as an agricultural adviser in India, published his *Agricultural Testament*. He claimed, from his observation of peoples in India, that in those areas in which animal manures and vegetable composts were carefully conserved and returned to the soil, and where the soils were well cultivated, drained and aerated, the people were active and outstandingly healthy; whereas in those areas in which people ate polished rice and much refined and processed food which had been grown with the aid of 'chemicals', they suffered from disease, parasites and malnutrition. It was an easy step to extend this argument to the Britain of the 1930s, in which bad teeth, rickets, anaemia and constipation were prevalent among the poorer classes and indeed among the population in general. Howard was undoubtedly right in stressing the virtues of fresh unadulterated food, but he also believed that manure, compost and humus improved the health and the resistance to disease of plants, animals and men, and that artificial fertilisers, by contrast, left them open to attack by disease and parasites of all sorts. He claimed, for instance, that insecticides and fungicides are unnecessary in traditional organic methods of agriculture.

Scientists no longer think his views are even worth discussing, for his ideas were loosely expressed and were backed by little evidence except his own personal observation. And yet in 'health food' shops in Britain and the USA, plenty of people are prepared to pay extra money for flour, fruit and vegetables which have been 'organically' grown without the use of artificials or pesticides. Many British farmers still believe that there is 'nothing like muck' and many British gardeners pay a high price for manures, dried blood and bone-meal in the belief that these will produce higher quality produce than artificials. And some there are indeed who believe that most of the ills of civilisation, from cancer and arthritis to foot-and-mouth disease, are the result of food having been 'poisoned' by chemical fertilisers.

Soil chemists on the other hand point out that there is no clear distinction between organic and inorganic fertilisers. (To the chemist a product is organic if it contains carbon – which has nothing to do with the usual distinctions between 'artificial' and 'natural' fertilisers.) If urea is separated from urine, for example, it cannot be distinguished chemically from synthetic urea. And plants do not absorb complex substances such as manures, but ions; and an ion of nitrogen derived from manure will be just the same as an ion of nitrogen derived from a synthetic fertiliser.

EFFECT OF FERTILISER ON QUALITY

Is there any real evidence then that apart from sheer yield or quantity, crops grown with natural manures are superior in quality to crops grown with artificials? The fact is that no one knows. The housewife, when she buys fruit or vegetables, can know little of their vitamin or mineral content but will be influenced by their colour, firmness and freshness. The vitamin content of fruit and vegetables in fact depends more on freshness, crop variety and climate than on the amount and kind of fertiliser used. It is certainly true that young beans, potatoes or carrots fresh from the home garden have a flavour that is very rare in the commercial article, in the same way that a young chicken reared on grass and clover is immeasurably superior to the insipid and often revolting product of the broiler industry.

Good farmyard manure is a balanced plant food which contains all the micronutrients so often lacking in artificials. Now, man needs many of the same micronutrients for his body functions as plants do for theirs. Of course he has the advantage of a much more varied diet than a plant. But if the vegetables he eats are short of calcium, phosphorus, iron and copper, his own physiology may well suffer, just as the plant's does.

Most of the criticism of artificials centres on nitrogen, especially if it is used alone. There is much resistance to fertiliser nitrogen among livestock farmers. They observe that grass fertilised with nitrogen alone often seems unpalatable to animals and that it can produce digestive disorders. It is also known that nitrogen is bad for the cooking quality of potatoes for human consumption: it leads to blackening after cooking and to loss of mealiness and flavour. From plant physiology it is also known that ammonia nitrogen depresses the uptake of calcium, magnesium and potassium, and that nitrates depress the phosphorus uptake. In general it is clear that the proper proportions of nutrients in the plant

H

can be upset by the application of large dressings of fertiliser nitrogen unbalanced by other elements.

Most commercial growers, being in business for profit, are more interested in the quantity of produce per acre than in its content of minerals, since these are not obvious to the eye. The fact is that we know very little of the mineral composition of the foods we eat. But until more evidence is available, home gardeners might well be cautious in the use of fertiliser nitrogen alone on food crops. We usually eat fresh fruit and vegetables, not for their protein or carbohydrate content, but for the vitamins and minerals they contain. Many diets are deficient in calcium and iron. One of the arguments for eating cabbage, garden beans, carrots and celery is that they are good sources of the calcium and phosphorus which are needed for growth. Therefore it is wrong to dress such crops with sulphate of ammonia which may depress their calcium content.

All authorities agree on the many virtues of manures and composts, and on the need to build up organic matter in the soil. We know that the unbalanced use of artificials sometimes does harm to farm stock, and that they are used mainly because they are economical and give high yields. In the present state of knowledge the lesson for home gardeners is, I think, that animal and green manures should be used as much as possible on crops for human consumption, and that fertiliser nitrogen should be properly balanced by other nutrients.

And taking a wider view, the large-scale use of inorganic nitrogen is turning clear streams and lakes into foul and turbid waters. As much as half of applied nitrogen finds its way into streams and rivers, where it encourages the growth of algae and bacteria. The water becomes deoxygenated so that fish and water-plants cannot live in it, and it becomes potentially dangerous to drink. There is therefore an added reason for avoiding the excessive use of inorganic nitrogen.

CHAPTER 6

ORGANIC MATTER

The stable yields a stercoraceous heap
Impregnated with quick fermenting salts
(Cowper)

THE FORMATION OF HUMUS

When plant remains are returned to the soil, they are decomposed by the soil microbes. The microbes consume the starches and some of the proteins, but in the process they liberate, for fresh use by plants, nitrogen, phosphorus, potassium, calcium and other nutrients. It is also thought that they produce acids which help to release some of the soil's stock of mineral nutrients.

The soil microbes need nitrogen for their activity. If plant residues are to feed both microbes and new plants, they need to contain at least 1·5 per cent of nitrogen. If material such as straw, or the coarse stems of plants, or peat, which contain little nitrogen, is added to the soil, the amount of available nitrogen may actually be reduced; for the microbes, unable to get enough nitrogen from the plant remains, draw on some of the soil's stock of nitrogen. Legume foliage, on the other hand, being high in nitrogen, can not only feed the microbes but also provide nitrogen for new growth.

Plant residues are finally broken down to a dark compound called humus, which consists of the harder and more woody remains in association with minerals and dead microbes. Much of it consists of the woody 'lignin' which resists microbial attack and is also able to bind proteins so that they cannot be decomposed. Humus too becomes closely bound to clay particles in the clay-humus complex, which holds important minerals in the soil and prevents them from being leached out. Much of the phosphorus available to plants and nearly all the soil's nitrogen exist in these organic compounds. The ratio of organic matter to nitrogen is fairly constant in most soils at about 20:1. So, if the nitrogen percentage in a soil is, say, 0·2 per cent, the total organic matter can be estimated to be about 4 per cent.

Humus is very closely mixed with the other soil constituents. It contains not only carbon, hydrogen, oxygen and nitrogen, but also the other nutrients such as phosphorus, potassium and calcium. Its great virtue is that it holds nutrients in the soil, so that they are protected from decomposition and leaching until the conditions are right for plant growth. For the same conditions which promote plant growth – temperature and moisture – also promote decomposition. Thus humus acts as a regulator of the rate of release of plant nutrients, releasing the nutrients in available form at the rate at which plants need them. This is its great advantage over inorganic fertilisers. It is easy to apply fertilisers in the wrong amounts at the wrong times. They have no similar mechanism to control their rate of release.

BENEFITS OF ORGANIC MATTER

The amount of organic matter in soils varies from nearly 100 per cent in peat bogs to near zero in desert sands. Old pastures or land that has been under grass may contain 3–4 per cent in the topsoil; most cultivated soils about 2–3 per cent. Clays and silts will contain more than sandy soils. For each kind of soil there is a natural limit to the organic content. Even after more than seventy years of heavy manuring, the organic content of arable soil does not rise more than about 0·5 per cent, say from 2 per cent to 2·5 per cent, and will never quite reach the high percentage found under permanent grass. But it is still important to build up organic matter, as an increase of only 0·5 per cent in the soil's organic content will greatly improve yields.

The main functions of organic matter are two:

1 to supply nutrients and to release them at the rate that plants require;
2 to improve soil structure, aeration and drainage.

The major plant nutrients can be supplied more cheaply by inorganic fertilisers even when, as usually happens, only a fraction of the amounts applied are actually used by plants. The main advantage of organic manures is that they can provide ample amounts of phosphorus and potassium to the seedling more safely and with less chance of damage than inorganic fertilisers. But, perhaps more important, few soils can do without the good aeration and drainage which organic matter gives.

Every observant gardener knows that soils which have had good dressings of farmyard manure are worked more easily and drain better. The clods break down more readily, while the soil has a 'crumb' structure and can be worked without much difficulty into a seed bed. A well-manured garden soil, cultivated when it is not too wet, 'digs well' and breaks down easily into fine crumbs of about $\frac{1}{8}$in. It will retain moisture. The surface does not readily form a hard crust. The young plant gets off to a good start, and root growth is easy.

Good garden loams naturally have this sort of structure. But after heavy rains, clays may become sticky, compacted and poorly drained; their surface slakes and crusts over. Fine sandy soils also become compacted and poorly aerated. In fine sand, therefore, organic matter is essential, and on clay highly desirable, to improve and open up the soil.

In addition to improving the physical structure of the soil, a good supply of organic matter diminishes the risk of disease. There is much evidence that high concentrations of soil nitrogen predispose plants to many diseases. When composts, manures and other organic residues are applied to the soil, the nitrates they contain encourage the growth of soil microbes, which take up all available nitrates and release them at a gradual and continuous rate. In this way undesirably high concentrations of nitrogen are avoided.

WAYS OF INCREASING ORGANIC MATTER

Over a period of years, garden soils lose much of their organic matter and nitrogen. Although the rate of loss becomes slower as time goes on, the organic matter falls after some twenty years to about 75 per cent of the original amount.

How then can the store of organic matter be built up? The main possibilities are:

1   to spade back all healthy plant remains and roots, chopping them up to speed decomposition;
2   to make compost and add it to the soil;
3   to add peat moss or leaf-mould;
4   to use green manures – that is, to grow a green crop and dig it in;
5   to put the land down to grass or lawn for a few seasons, and then dig it in;
6   to use farmyard manure.

I   DIGGING IN PLANT REMAINS

All or any of these methods will work fairly well in a good, established garden. The organic matter can be kept at a high level by growing good crops and making sure that the remains and the roots are well dug back into the soil. Yet many gardeners do not do this. In the interests of tidiness and neatness they carefully remove old plants and put them on their garden bonfires (thus adding to the smoke pall which covers so many suburban gardens on fine summer afternoons). When plant remains are burnt, the nitrogen and sulphur they contain are lost as gases. Other nutrients such as phosphorus and potassium remain in the ash, but in such a form that they are easily washed out by rains before they can be taken up again by plants. Clearing and burning also results in a decline in the humus content of soils. In continuous arable farming, where livestock are not kept, this is the main method of keeping up the organic matter: to plough back the stubbles and crop remains in the autumn. But this method will not help much if a garden is too poor to grow good crops in the first place; although, incidentally, the more luxuriant garden weeds are worth growing if they can be chopped and spaded back into the soil before they have seeded.

2 COMPOST

It is also unlikely that garden compost will be of much help in a poor garden. To make good compost, fairly large quantities of plant refuse are needed.

Unless there is enough vegetable refuse to make a heap of compost about 9ft × 5ft × 5ft, one is unlikely to succeed in making good compost in cool climates. Such a quantity of plant remains can come only from a garden of half an acre or more in size. Even in a large heap, decomposition is much slower in temperate than in tropical countries. The organisms which break down the plant remains are inactive at temperatures under 10° C and are most active at temperatures over 20° C. In temperate zones, soil heats up to these levels only in summer. Heat is conserved better in a pit than in a heap – a pit can be smaller than a heap – but some labour is involved in digging out a pit of the size required. Moreover, in a wet summer a pit needs to be covered and well drained so that it does not become waterlogged. Nevertheless, many frugal gardeners compost their kitchen and garden waste in a small pit, and although the final product may not be always sweet humus, at least vegetable wastes eventually find their way back to the soil. As an alternative to a pit, a rectangular structure with boarded sides will also conserve heat in cool climates. Small boarded 'bins' of this type are probably the most satisfactory receptacles in small gardens where no great quantities of plant material are available at any one time.

If there is not enough waste to make a satisfactory pit or heap, such substances as straw or brewer's grains can be bought in sufficient quantities to make a heap which will ferment. Materials can include all vegetable and crop remains such as annual weeds, grass, hedge trimmings, straw and kitchen waste (but not potato peel). Leaves, twigs and woody stems decompose very slowly and are best left out. All the materials should be chopped and crushed. Fresh green leaves need to be wilted and soft waste such as lawn mowings should be mixed with coarser material, otherwise silage instead of compost may result.

The pit or heap is then built of the mixed materials in layers of 6in of crop refuse topped by 2in of animal manure, followed

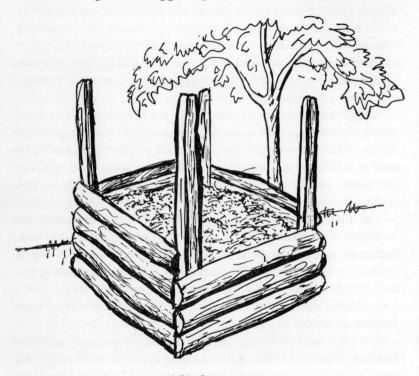

A bin for compost

by a few shovelfuls of earth sprinkled with lime. Further layers are built up until the heap is 4–5ft high, when it is covered with 4–5in of soil. If animal manures are not available a mixture of fertiliser salts including nitrogen is used instead, a few handfuls being sprinkled on each layer. The layers can be added one at a time or the entire heap built at once, depending on the supply of material.

Success depends on moisture, air, temperature and a carbon/ nitrogen ratio in the composted material which will encourage rapid decomposition. The material must be wet but not soaked. To aerate the heap, it should not be too compact (but not too loose either). Grass trimmings are the only material which may be too compacted. Stakes may be driven down to aerate the heap. A high enough temperature can be ensured in temperate countries only in summer, and then only by making a heap of about 200cu ft. Nitrogen is supplied in the form of either animal manure or artificial nitrogen. Straw or other woody material will need more added nitrogen than ordinary garden refuse, 1cwt of straw needing about 2lb of nitrogen.

After three weeks or so the pile should begin to heat up and steam. At this stage the material is covered with a greyish-white mildew. The heap should then be turned so that the outside goes inside. After about three to four months, given warm weather, the heap should be transformed into sweet-smelling brown humus.

The main causes of failure are likely to be over-acidity (insufficient lime), too much moisture in wet climates and temperatures too low to allow of enough microbial activity. Special starters or activators can be purchased. These may contain bacteria which can work at a lower temperature than normal. But it will usually be just as effective to add well-rotted manure or some sods from an old pasture.

In a cool wet summer, compost-making is not easy; and it is certainly a forlorn hope to put couch-grass and bindweed in the heap in the hope that it will heat up to 75° C and destroy them. The best compromise for most gardeners is a small pit or bin for such kitchen and garden waste as cannot be immediately dug into the soil.

Composting has no real advantage over letting plant material rot down in the soil itself, unless the temperature of the heap can be raised to such a heat that weed seeds and insect pests are destroyed. If this is not possible, plant materials may just as well be spaded back to rot in the ground. This is of course not always convenient, and during the summer months when the ground is full of plants, every garden has a 'rubbish' heap – in which good organic matter is too often wasted or burnt. On clay soils particularly, where the soil needs opening up, it may be better to dig plant remains straight into the soil than to leave them in a rubbish heap.

3   PEAT

Perhaps the easiest, but also the most expensive, way of adding organic matter is to dig in quantities of peat. But this substance, although improving the physical properties of soils, adds little in the way of nutrients.

Peat represents the accumulation of plant remains over centuries. It is found in boggy areas in which plant remains have failed to decompose because they have been covered with water: in a waterlogged soil there is not sufficient oxygen for decomposition. Thus peat starts forming around the edges of shallow lakes.

The two main forms of garden peat are moss or sphagnum peat, and the more fibrous sedge or reed peats. Peat is not standard but varies in the nature of the original vegetation, in its degree of decomposition and in the conditions under which it was formed.

Moss or sphagnum peats are usually very acid, with a pH of about 4. They contain only about 1 per cent of nitrogen and only minute amounts of other nutrients. They are spongy in texture and hold about twenty times their own weight of water.

Sedge peats are usually less acid, having a pH between 5 and 7. They contain about 2 per cent of nitrogen, but little in the way of other nutrients. They are more fibrous and contain more lignin-like substances than moss peats. They hold about five times their own weight of water.

All peats are sterile and resist microbial decomposition. If they are used as a substitute for farmyard manure, it is clear that, while they improve the aeration of all soils and the water-retention of sandy soils, they supply practically no nutrients. Indeed, since moss peat is so low in nitrogen, its incorporation in the soil may lead to an actual drop in the supply of nitrogen available to plants, and it therefore needs to be supplemented by nitrogen from some other source.

In seed and potting composts, peat is included to increase water-retention and aeration. For composts which contain loam, fibrous granulated peat, sieved if necessary to granules of ⅛–⅜in, is suitable. For loamless composts which contain only sand and peat, greater water-retention is provided by moss peat of higher water-holding capacity.

The more acid moss peats are, of course, preferred for calcifuge plants. For most purposes the lighter, more fibrous peats are preferable to the darker, more decomposed types.

On lighter soils, which lack organic matter, fibrous peat may be applied at the rate of 1–2cwt per rod. During the growing season it is often used as a mulch which is later spaded into the topsoil. All peat needs to be thoroughly wetted before use. The finer sorts are difficult to wet when they have dried out, and may need to be soaked.

4   GREEN MANURING AND CATCH-CROPPING

There is some doubt as to whether green manuring – that is, growing a green crop such as mustard or clover or lupins and digging it into the soil when still green – adds much organic matter to the soil. But it is a useful practice because (1) it prevents nutrients from being washed out of the soil, (2) a deep-rooted green crop will also 'mine' minerals from the subsoil and make them more available and (3) if a legume is grown, nitrogen will be added to the soil.

Green manuring is most needed in hungry sandy soils from which winter rainfall will drain the nutrients if the soil is left bare. Such soils should have an overwinter cover – even weeds are better than nothing – to prevent leaching. To be successful, a green manure crop has to be thick and bulky and quick-growing. It is in fact much easier to green manure well in warm countries, where plants grow fast and also rapidly decompose in the soil.

Mustard is a crop which makes quick growth and is often

used. And winter rye is useful since it will make some growth whenever the ground is not frozen. Such crops need to be sown not later than August, in order for them to be established before the winter. The seed should be broadcast thickly and dressed with plenty of mixed fertiliser or manure.

Green manures are best turned into the soil in spring, but unless the spring is warm and the plant material young and leafy, some six to eight weeks will be needed before the crop decomposes and another one can be sown; for the soil microbes which decompose the remains make the same sort of demands on the soil as the new plant growth. Certainly, if much woody cellulose has to be broken down, the microbes will compete with the crop for nitrogen. In such cases extra fertiliser should be applied with the green manure in order to feed the soil bacteria and the new crop.

The length of time that it is necessary to wait between turning in the green manure and sowing the new crop will depend on the carbon/nitrogen ratio of the green manure and on the soil temperature. A leafy legume will be decomposed in the soil within a few days if the weather is hot. A mature stemmy crop of a non-legume may take eight weeks or more to decompose in the early spring before the ground has warmed up.

In practice, there are two important roles for green manure in the garden: (1) a clover or legume can be sown in spring and turned in in July or August on ground intended for winter greens, which need plenty of nitrogen, (2) a cover crop such as mustard or rye can be sown in late summer to conserve nutrients and prevent them from being leached by winter rains.

If land cannot be spared for the rather long period needed for green manuring, it may be possible to intersow a green manure with a main crop, to grow a green manure on a small plot and use some of the top growth on other plots, or to sow wild white clover in a lawn and compost or dig in the lawn mowings.

5   PUTTING DOWN LAND TO GRASS

The last course – that of putting down land to grass and clovers –

will result in the biggest increase in organic matter. This is the garden equivalent of ley farming. If the grass is mown at intervals and the cuttings are not removed but are left on the ground, much plant residue in time is incorporated into the top soil.

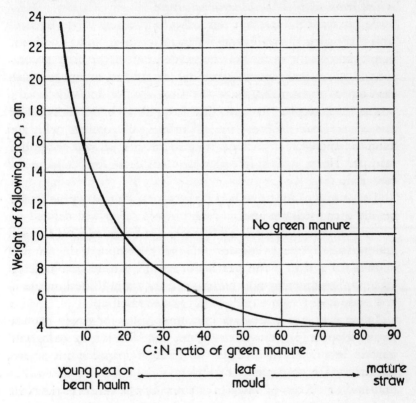

Composition of green manure and its effect on growth of following crop

For this purpose perennial rye grass provides more roots and more bulk than most other grasses.

In effect, this means putting down an area to rough lawn for perhaps two or three years, and then turning the sod in. But, although gardeners are patient people, few probably can think on this sort of time-scale or have a garden layout which would lend itself to being grassed down in this fashion.

6 FARMYARD MANURE

(a) *Composition* Farmyard manure is still much valued by farmers and market gardeners; and their belief in the virtues of 'muck' is based on first-hand observation of its beneficial action. Well-made farmyard manure not only adds organic matter to the soil but is a complete and reasonably balanced fertiliser. Some gardeners may think that it is bulky, expensive and offensive. But well-rotted manure is not unpleasant to use and it is no more expensive than other organic manures.

The composition of farmyard manure is very variable. It depends on the kind of animals it comes from, on how the animals have been fed and on the sort of litter used to make the manure. Horse and sheep manures are drier and more con-centrated than the manure of cattle or pigs; they contain less moisture. Horse manure especially is 'warmer' and ferments more readily than cattle manure.

Phosphate is excreted in the faeces, but much of the nitrogen and potash in the urine. In well-made manure, urine is not allowed to run to waste but is absorbed by the litter. Indeed, dung without litter is not manure and will be lacking in potash.

The dung of young animals is not as rich in nitrogen, phosphate and lime as that of mature beasts, because more of these minerals are used up in growth. Similarly, the manure of dairy cows will contain less nutrients than that of bullocks, since nutrients are needed for the production of milk.

(b) *Analysis* Average values for some of the main nutrients in farmyard manure are:

	Nitrogen %	Phosphorus %	Potassium %	Calcium %	Moisture %
Bullock	0·6	0·12	0·7	0·3	80
Cow	0·4	0·1	0·4	0·2	85
Horse	0·6	0·1	0·5	0·2	75
Pig	0·4	0·1	0·5	0·1	80
Poultry	1·0	0·4	0·6	0·4	60
Sheep	0·8	0·1	0·7	0·3	60

The nutrient ratio of well-made cow or bullock manure is approximately 5:1:5, and this is very close to the ratio in which the major nutrients are required by plants. Since plants and grazing animals have been living together for some millions of years, it would indeed by surprising if this were not the case. Nitrogen and potash are supplied in about equal amounts; phosphorus is only about one-fifth of either the nitrogen or the potash. But this is about the right proportion of phosphorus, since many crops remove about 20lb of phosphorus per acre as against about 100lb each of nitrogen and potassium. It used to be thought that farmyard manure did not supply enough phosphorus to meet the needs of plants, and farmers were advised to sprinkle superphosphate on their manure heap. This was to have the double function of supplying extra phosphate and of fixing nitrogen. Nowadays it is thought that the nitrogen fraction of farmyard manure is the one which perhaps needs supplementing, and that farmyard manure provides enough phosphorus and potassium to meet the needs of most crops.

To supply these amounts of nutrients, fairly large amounts of manure are required. One per cent of a ton is 22·4lb, and since phosphorus constitutes only about 0·1 per cent of manure, some 10 tons per acre would be needed to meet the requirements of an acre of garden crops – that is, 100lb nitrogen, 20lb phosphorus and 100lb potassium.

(c) *Trace elements* It might appear that it would be much cheaper and easier to spread 5cwt of sulphate of ammonia (20 per cent nitrogen), 3cwt superphosphate (7 per cent phosphorus) and 2½cwt of sulphate of potash (40 per cent potassium) rather than 10 tons of manure. But manure is a complete fertiliser in a way that artificials are not. All the plant nutrients find their way through the animal's digestive system to the manure, and therefore the manure should contain some of the minor and trace elements present in the original food; manure contains not only nitrogen, phosphorus and potassium but also lime, magnesium and the trace elements.

Farmyard manure has fair quantities of all the micronutrients

Average percentage in dry matter

Nitrogen	N	2·0	
Phosphorus	P	0·4	
Potassium	K	1·7	
Calcium	Ca	0·74	
Magnesium	Mg	0·34	
Manganese	Mn	0·0002	(200ppm)
Boron	B	0·00008	(80ppm)
Copper	Cu	0·00002	(20ppm)
Zinc	Zn	0·00004	(40ppm)
Molybdenum	Mo	0·000002	(2ppm)

and the simplest way of overcoming many deficiencies is to give a dressing of it. By contrast, synthetic nitrogen and potash fertilisers have few or none of the micronutrients. Superphosphate contains some, but farmyard manure remains a much better source, particularly of manganese, which of all the trace elements is perhaps the one most frequently deficient in horticulture.

(*d*) *Other advantages of farmyard manure*   In addition to its chemical composition, farmyard manure has many other attributes:

1   it improves the soil structure, ensuring better aeration and drainage of heavy soils, and binding together light soils;
2   it helps soils to hold moisture and to withstand drought;
3   it is slow-acting, and releases nutrients gradually, at rates which match the needs of growing plants; in particular it supplies phosphorus and potassium to the seedling in large but not toxic amounts;
4   it encourages earthworms, and the soil microbes and fungi, many of which enhance soil fertility;
5   it has been proved to be better than nitrogen, phosphorus and potassium fertilisers for many vegetables. Red beet, runner beans, peas, leeks, spring cabbage, lettuce and potatoes are especially responsive to farmyard manure. The richness of good farmyard manure in available potash is one of the reasons for its effectiveness on these crops.

(*e*) *The rotting of manure*   When fresh manure is applied to the soil, there is a period of 'nitrogen starvation' when the soil microbes use all the available soil nitrogen while they feed on the straw litter. If manure is left to ferment in a heap, it loses about half its dry matter. This older well-rotted manure is more concentrated than fresh manure, but unfortunately it usually loses its nutrients while it is rotting in a heap. If it is not covered, rainfall will wash out the nutrients (even when covered, some seepage of nutrients will occur) and if the heap is loosely and poorly made, nitrogen will be volatilised and lost. The best manure will therefore come from a tight heap made under cover on a concrete standing which does not allow nutrients to seep away into the ground.

Most gardeners prefer to use well-rotted manure because it is easier to handle and spread and is in better mechanical condition. Also, fresh manure in which the nitrogen is highly available may 'burn' growing plants. There is no danger of this when the manure is rotted.

In rotted manure, some nitrogen is lost but the phosphorus is more soluble. When manure is being applied well in advance of sowing, there is no advantage in rotting it other than for ease of handling. When it is applied as a dressing or a mulch to growing plants, on the other hand, it will be safer if it has been rotted.

RATE AND METHOD OF APPLICATION OF
FARMYARD MANURE

In commercial horticulture in which the ground is cropped intensively, potatoes and vegetables receive up to 30 tons of farmyard manure per acre annually. This is equivalent to almost 4cwt per sq rod or about 15lb per sq yd. Except when used as a mulch, manure should be dug well into the soil. It must not remain on the surface or be buried so shallowly that it will dry out. In digging, manure is usually forked into the trench and well covered as the digging proceeds.

Farmyard manure will lose much of its ammonia nitrogen if it is left lying on the surface of the ground. As much as 25 per cent of the total nitrogen may be lost in a single day. This loss results

I

from drying out by the wind or from washing out by rain. If possible, therefore, manure should be applied under dry and windless conditions.

Manure should not be left on the garden in small heaps exposed to the sun, wind and rain. Not only will ammonia volatilise, but the manure will also go mouldy. And if it rains, nutrients will be washed into the underlying soil, leading to rank uneven growth.

The best time to dig in well-rotted manure is shortly before planting time. Manure will be wasted if it is dug into light sandy soils in the autumn. In clays and more retentive soils this is not so important. But if the manure is fresh and contains straw which has not rotted down, it should be dug in some months before sowing to give it time to decompose.

SUBSTITUTES FOR FARMYARD MANURE

Substitutes for farmyard manure include dried cow manure and spent mushroom compost. Dried cow manure should contain the same quantity of nutrients as about five times its weight of farmyard manure, which holds around 80 per cent moisture. Dried cow manure is reputed to have an analysis of 2 per cent nitrogen, 1·5 per cent phosphorus and 2 per cent potassium as against the 0·4 per cent nitrogen, 1 per cent phosphorus and 0·4 per cent potassium of farmyard manure. But if the dried manure does not contain litter, it is likely that much of the potash present in the urine will have been lost, and that the product will be inferior to the traditional manure.

Spent mushroom compost is a mixture of about 50 per cent horse manure or artificially treated straw and 50 per cent of clay casing soil from mushroom beds. Its nutrient value is likely to be small, but it should provide a useful supply of organic matter especially on sandy soils.

CHAPTER 7

LIME

... the strong clay of Essex and Suffolk is made
fruitful by the soft meliorating melting chalk of
Kent, which fattens and enriches it.

(Defoe)

SOIL REACTION

Soils can be acid or neutral or alkaline, depending largely on the
amount of calcium and other exchangeable cations they contain.
The acidity-alkalinity of a soil is called the soil reaction. Although
most plants will grow well in a slightly acid soil, and some indeed
prefer an acid soil, lime needs to be added at intervals to most of
the soils of humid regions to sweeten them and to make them less
acid.

Acid soils are most prevalent in districts of high rainfall.
The main causes of acidity are (1) that the parent materials of
the soil were acid and contained little calcium and (2) that heavy
rainfall has leached calcium downwards in the soil, washing it
out of the reach of plants. In the humid climate of Northern
Europe, for example, the natural vegetation is forest, and in the
natural cycle of leaf-fall, decomposition and new uptake, calcium
and other nutrients are conserved. But when the trees are cleared
and replaced by arable land, calcium is lost in drainage; for
although limestone is insoluble in pure water, it is dissolved if
water contains carbon dioxide. Soil water does contain carbon
dioxide and this is the main cause of surface soils losing their
calcium, the calcium being replaced by hydrogen ions.

Limestone, an impure form of calcium carbonate, is the most

common state in which calcium exists in nature. In the early days of the earth, calcium was dissolved and carried out to sea. There it was deposited on the seabed and some of it was used by small marine creatures for their shells and skeletons. In time these deposits became rock and were eventually thrown up in great earthquakes to become the chalk and limestone hills of today. Much of England, for example, has been several times submerged, the last time being some 120 million years ago, when the great chalk deposits of the South were laid down.

Natural vegetation varies with the amount of calcium in the soil. On chalk the natural vegetation includes beech, dogwood, hazel, traveller's joy and old man's beard; and among flowering plants, the vetches, bird's-foot trefoil, burnet, sheep's scabious and gentians. At the other extreme, acid soils support an entirely different flora: conifers, sessile oaks, heather, heath, bilberry, furze and foxgloves. As a result of the long ages of adaptation to environment, most of the chalk flora will not grow in acid soils nor will the plants of acid moorland grow on chalk.

The greater number of plants, however, will grow well over a fair range of soil reaction. Most garden plants thrive in a slightly acid soil; but there are exceptions. Lime-loving plants (calciphiles) will not thrive in acid soils and lime-hating plants (calcifuges), such as rhododendrons, will not thrive on chalk or limestone. In the ordinary garden, soil reaction can seldom be fitted exactly to the plant nor, within limits, is it necessary to do so except in the special case of definite calciphiles and calcifuges. The soil of pots and greenhouse beds, on the other hand, can and should be adapted to the preferences of the plant. Also, since nearly all garden vegetables dislike acid soils, vegetable gardens should receive regular dressings of lime.

THE pH SCALE

Soil reaction is usually measured on the pH scale.

On this scale the value 7·0 indicates the neutral mid-point, which is the pH of pure water. The pH of soils ranges from about 3·0 on the very acid moors to about 8·0 on chalk or lime-

stone, and to even higher figures on alkaline soils. But most are
in the range 4·5–7·0.

The pH scale is a logarithmic scale: pH6 is ten times more acid
than pH7; pH5 ten times more acid than pH6; and so on. Thus,

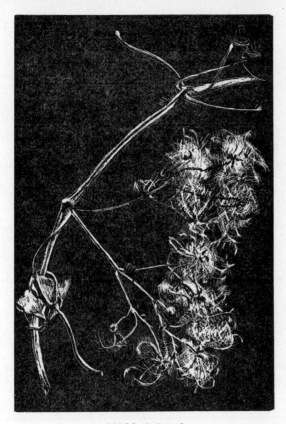

Old Man's Beard

although there is very little acidity or alkalinity in the range
pH6–8, outside this range the increase in both is very great.
Below pH5·5, many chemical changes occur in the soil which
interfere with the growth of all but acid-adapted flora.

Soils may be classified according to their pH values as follows:

Extremely acid   less than pH4·5
Acid   pH4·6–5·5
Slightly acid   pH5·6–6·5
Neutral or near neutral   pH6·6–7·5
Slightly alkaline   pH7·6–8·5
Alkaline   above pH8·5

Below pH4 and above pH9 acidity and alkalinity are directly injurious to plants. At pH values above 6·5, iron and some trace elements precipitate from solution and are deposited in insoluble form. But at pH values below 5·5, phosphates become unavailable and aluminium and manganese, which are toxic to many species, become soluble. The majority of plants, therefore, will do best in the middle range around pH6, at which the essential elements are most available.

To some extent rain decreases acidity, so that plants are less affected by acidity in cool moist conditions than they are in hotter, drier conditions.

MEASURING SOIL pH

Some idea of the acidity of a soil can be formed without measuring the pH. The heavier the rainfall and the sandier the soil, the more likely is the soil to be acid. It is said that an acid soil actually tastes acid when applied to the tongue. Natural vegetation provides some clues to soil reaction. Some weeds are fairly reliable indicators of acidity. Profuse growth of sheep's sorrel in the garden suggests an acid soil; in grass the absence of clovers, and the prevalence of such grasses as Yorkshire fog and bent. Lime-loving wild plants whose presence shows absence of acidity include kidney vetch, bird's-foot trefoil and the climbing plant old man's beard (*Clematis vitalba*).

There are two main methods of measuring soil pH:

1   electrical, using a pH meter with a glass electrode (this is the usual laboratory method);
2   colorimetric, using various indicator dyes. This method is commonly employed in the field or garden. Small test kits are readily available.

Sheep's Sorrel

Litmus paper which turns red in acid and blue in alkali is a familiar indicator. There are many others in which the colour of the indicator when added to a solution changes with the degree of acidity, thus indicating the pH value. Most soil test kits contain indicators which change colour gradually over a wide pH range. A small amount of soil is shaken with a measured quantity of distilled water; the indicator is then added to the suspension and the colour of the suspension is identified on a graded colour chart.

The reliability of measurements of this kind is affected by (1) fluctuations in the soil pH and (2) actual errors of measurement.

Soil pH fluctuates with the seasons. Acidity increases from spring to midsummer, being accentuated in dry periods. Rain decreases acidity. By early winter the soil pH returns to the spring level. Since it usually takes at least six months to rectify soil acidity, tests are most conveniently made in the autumn so that lime can be applied before the winter sets in.

In taking samples of soil for testing, results can be falsified if the soil is removed from the site of a bonfire or from close to a place where a hole has been dug in the ground. A high salt concentration resulting from fertiliser residues will also lower the measured pH. To avoid such sources of error, several samples need to be taken from different parts of a garden.

Errors can also result when the glass or chinaware used in tests is not kept perfectly clean, and when the indicator dyes deteriorate with storage.

From all these considerations it is evident that there is much scope for error, and to get some idea of the accuracy of measurement it is as well to test pH by using two soil test kits of different make which employ different kinds of indicator. If they agree reasonably well, some confidence can be placed in the result. But without at least two independent measurements, the result may be untrustworthy.

CHEMICAL EFFECTS

Soils become acid because, through long periods of time, rainwater percolating down through the soil washes out calcium and magnesium. The calcium and magnesium are replaced by hydrogen ions carried by the water. When a soil is limed, calcium once again replaces hydrogen.

A pH reading of, say, 5·0 means only one part of acid hydrogen in 1 million, which seems unlikely to damage plants. But the pH reading is only an estimate of the active, not the total or potential, acidity. In acid soils, humus and clay particles hold a large stock of hydrogen and aluminium in the form of exchangeable cations, and as the hydrogen ions in the soil solution are neutralised, these exchangeable cations leave the particle surfaces and enter the soil solution. In this way soils are buffered against changes in pH.

At low soil pH, potentially toxic elements such as aluminium and manganese become more soluble and may be taken up in large amounts. Aluminium occurs in acid soil in great quantity. The soluble aluminium in a soil may rise from 0·2ppm at pH5·5 to 15ppm at pH4·5 – a seventy-five fold increase in one pH unit. Many plants are poisoned by more than 1ppm of aluminium. Onions and lettuce are especially sensitive.

But pH has its most striking effect on the availability of plant nutrients.

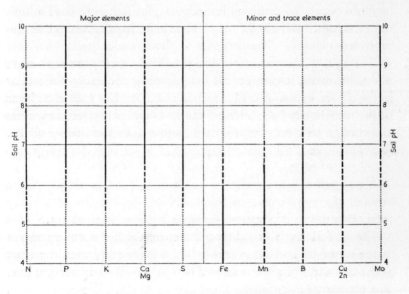

The influence of pH on the availability of nutrients

The diagram shows that the major elements are only sparingly available below about pH5·5; but that the minor elements, except molybdenum, are all poorly available above about pH7·0. There is therefore a fairly narrow range, centred at pH6·5, over which all the elements are freely available.

So the effect of soil acidity is mostly indirect. Its damaging effects result from the major nutrients becoming less available, and other elements such as aluminium or manganese becoming available in harmfully large amounts.

When plants are grown in soilless cultures (water culture) they thrive under very acid conditions. This proves that it is not acidity itself which is harmful, but the effects which it has in upsetting the balance of nutrients in the soil. As soils become more acid, deficiencies of the major nutrients begin to occur, accompanied by harmfully large amounts of some minor and trace elements and of aluminium. At the other extreme, as soils become alkaline, deficiencies of the minor and trace elements begin to occur. Azaleas and hydrangeas, for instance, have a high need for iron. But as soils become less acid, iron becomes increasingly less soluble. Therefore, these plants which grow perfectly well in an alkaline water solution provided they get enough iron, will not flourish in chalk soils. Iron deficiency likewise may occur in fruit-trees growing on limestone soils. And in soils that have been over-limed, iron, manganese and boron become insoluble and enough of these elements is therefore not absorbed by plants.

CALCIUM AS A PLANT FOOD

The pH value can usually be taken as a reliable index of the amount of available calcium in a soil. But in some sandy and peaty soils calcium can be short, even when pH is as high as 5·5.

The typical signs of calcium deficiency are: the young leaves at the terminal bud become hooked downwards, then die back at the tips and margins, followed by death of the growing points. The premature fall of flowers can also be a sign of lack of calcium. These symptoms appear fairly often in newly transplanted specimens, and in pot plants grown in peat without the addition of lime. They usually go unrecognised.

In the vegetable garden, brassicas and legumes are especially susceptible to calcium shortage, cabbage in particular taking up large amounts of calcium. Fruit-trees – apples, cherries and peaches – are also large consumers. And tomato and potato plants

also contain much calcium. In tomatoes, calcium shortage causes
blossom end rot (black sunken areas at the far end of the fruit).
In potatoes, multiple or 'satellite' tubers are formed.

These troubles can be quickly set right by spraying the leaves
with dilute lime water, and by watering in lime to the soil around
the roots.

ADVANTAGES OF LIME

Lime, chalk and marl have been applied to farmland for many
centuries. In districts where chalk was readily available, as much
as 50 tons per acre were sometimes applied. This was done
mainly because chalk improved the working qualities of clay
soils, opening them up and making them more porous and easier
to till. On lighter soils lime prevented the surface soil from crust-
ing over. Lime was used largely because it improved the physical
texture of soils.

An old gardening belief was that lime was a soil-steriliser and
insecticide; that it helped to keep down soilborne diseases and
destroyed insects. Unfortunately, there is little foundation for this
belief, which is still held by many gardeners.

The advantages of liming acid soils are:

1   In line with traditional practice, it improves the physical condition of the soil. Clay soils in particular become better drained
and aerated, and their clods break up more easily.
2   It provides calcium as a plant food, replaces calcium which
has been lost from the soil, and adds to the soil reserves of calcium.
3   It makes other elements such as phosphorus more available to
plants. In acid soils, below $pH 5 \cdot 5$, phosphorus unites with
aluminium and iron in insoluble compounds. When soils are
limed, less phosphorus is fixed in these insoluble forms.
4   The bacteria which produce nitrate and those which fix
nitrogen work better at a pH above $6 \cdot 0$. Liming the soil increases
their activity, and more nitrogen is therefore freed for plant
use.

Lime also encourages earthworms, which are thought to be beneficial because they aerate the soil. There are few earthworms in very acid soils, below pH4·5.

5   Lime prevents aluminium and manganese from being taken up in excess. Acid soils contain large amounts of soluble aluminium and manganese, which some plants cannot tolerate. Onions, lettuce and celery are especially sensitive to excess aluminium; cauliflower and french beans to too great amounts of manganese. In excess, aluminium and manganese accumulate in the plant and interfere with the uptake of other nutrients. Lime makes aluminium and manganese insoluble and harmless.

6   Lime reduces the excess intake or 'luxury consumption' of potash. All plants will absorb more potash than they need. But when lime is applied, more calcium and less potash is taken up. Since calcium is such an important element in both human and animal diets, and is often deficient, it is desirable that vegetables and food crops should contain a high level of calcium.

7   Lime reduces the chances of the fungus of club-root (finger and toe disease) in the cabbage family. This is a fungus disease which does not occur above pH6. Lime does not cure the disease, but it is a preventive.

Lime can also do harm. If soils are limed over a period of years without manures also being supplied, soil fertility is depleted; for since lime speeds up the decomposition of humus and releases other minerals, more nutrients need to be put back into the soil in replacement.

LOSSES OF CALCIUM FROM THE SOIL

In areas in which the rainfall is over 30in per annum, some 1–2cwt per acre of calcium is leached out of soils by rain each year. Fertilisers such as sulphate of ammonia also make the soil acid by displacing calcium. Using 100lb of sulphate of ammonia causes a loss of about the same amount of calcium carbonate. Using chloride of potash also results in a loss of calcium. Calcium is likewise removed in crops, but this loss is small in relation to that caused by rainfall and acid fertilisers.

Farmyard manure supplies calcium and reduces acidity a little. Deep-rooting crops also salvage some of the calcium that has been washed into the lower soil layers by rain. But in the wet climates, garden soils tend to lose their calcium and to become acid.

PLANT RESPONSE TO LIME – TABLES FOR VEGETABLES, FLOWERS AND SHRUBS

In the vegetable garden it is especially important to ensure that the soil is only slightly acid. At pH5·5, for example, the yield of vegetables may be only about 80 per cent of the optimum. At pH4·5 and below, some of them fail entirely. The yield of such crops as onions and beets can be raised many times when very acid soils are given adequate lime. It is therefore essential to correct the more extreme forms of acidity if most of the common garden vegetables are to be grown.

That lime vastly improves the yield of many plants on very acid soils is shown in the following table:

	Unlimed	*Limed*
Sweet pea (numbers of flowers)	780	3,433
Raspberry (red) (pounds of fruit)	6	12·8
Asparagus (pounds)	Nil	9·2
Beet (pounds)	0·2	164·2
Lettuce (pounds)	0·02	44·4
Onion (pounds)	0·3	41·5

(Rhode Island Experiment Station)

The four vegetables were total failures on the unlimed soils.

But acid-loving plants were found to thrive better on the unlimed than on the limed soil:

	Unlimed	*Limed*
Norway spruce		
(inches gained in diameter)	1·5	1·1
Blackberry		
(pounds of fruit)	5·1	3·2
Water-melon		
(pounds)	224	166

Beet, cabbage and cauliflower respond to lime even when the soil is not strongly acid. Legumes such as beans and peas are also responsive.

Many flowers, trees and shrubs are not quite as exacting in their requirements, and will grow well over a wide range of pH. The tables which follow set out the pH range over which common vegetables, flowers and shrubs will grow. They are included only as a general guide. The precise limits cannot be given with accuracy, for the limits will vary with climate and soil type. Moreover, the tables are based on consensus among authorities rather than on firm experimental evidence. But they are nevertheless useful, and indeed for important commercial crops, critical values below which the crop will not be a success have been accurately established. Some of these critical values, for humid climates, are:

pH5·0 Tomato, sweet corn
pH5·4 Cucumber
pH5·5 Bedding plants (as aster, salvia, gloxinia, zinnia), peas, beans, carrots, celery
pH5·6 Chrysanthemum
pH5·8 Carnation
pH6·0 Lettuce, onions, leeks, parsnips, antirrhinum
pH6·5 Cauliflower, spinach

Although nearly all vegetables, most flowers and the greater number of trees and shrubs will grow well in the pH range 5·5–6·5, there are exceptions at both ends of the scale. In a very acid soil at the one extreme, and in a chalk or limestone soil at the other, the best policy may be to choose plants which suit the local conditions, rather than to try to make great changes in the soil. The table shows the relative sensitivity of vegetables to acid soil conditions:

VEGETABLES

Very sensitive pH6·5–7·5	Sensitive pH6·7–5	Tolerant pH5·5–7·0	Very Tolerant pH5·0–6·0
Asparagus	Bean (french)	Broad bean	Potato
Beet	Broccoli	Cucumber	Rhubarb
Cauliflower	Cabbage	Brussels sprout	Strawberry
Celery	Chives	Kale	
Jerusalem	Cucumber	Marrow	
artichoke	Horseradish	Parsley	
Leek	Mustard	Raspberry	
Lettuce*	Parsnip	Swede	
Onion*	Pea	Sweet potato	
Spinach*	Pepper	Tomato	
Watercress	Radish	Water-melon	
	Sweet corn		
	Turnip		

* Especially sensitive to aluminium excess

All the common vegetables can be grown in a soil of pH6·5. This is true even of potatoes, but since potatoes suffer from scab at values above pH5·5, potato soils are usually not limed.

For the vegetables listed in the two left-hand columns the, liming of acid soils will usually be essential to good yields.

The tables on pp152–3 list the responses of flowers, shrubs and trees to acid soils. Roses are among the flowers which are fairly tolerant of soil acidity, geraniums among the most sensitive.

While the table holds good for most of the species in a genus, there are many exceptions. For instance, most heaths and heathers are calcifuges, but *Erica carnea* and *E. mediterranea* grow well on chalk. And among the normally calcifuge rhododendrons *Rhododendron hirsutum* is tolerant of less acid conditions.

Most conifers, as spruce, hemlock, larch, pine and fir prefer acid soils of pH4·5–5·0. Western Red Cedar prefers a less acid soil of pH5·5–6·5. Grecian Silver Fir (*Abies cepalonica*) and Spanish Fir (*A. pinsapo*) grow well on chalk.

Most hardwoods (including oak, beech, birch, sycamore) will

FLOWERS

Very sensitive pH6·5–7·5	*Sensitive* pH6·0–7·5	*Tolerant* pH5·5–7·0	*Very tolerant* pH5·0–6·0	*Acid-lovers* pH4·5–5·5
Amaranthus	Alyssum	Ageratum	Amaryllis	Aconite
Annual phlox	Aquilegia	Bulbs (most)	Aster	Anemones
(Drum-	Caillardia	Calceolaria	Begonia	(some)
mondii)	Candytuft	Calendula	Calliopsis	Autumn
Crocus	Carnation	Canna	Coreopsis	gentians
Flax	Cosmos	Chrysanthe-	Lawn grasses	Hydrangea
Forget-me-	Daffodil	mum	Lilies (most)	(blue)
not	Dahlia	Cineraria	Lupin	Iris
Geranium	Delphinium	Clarkia	Orchid	(Kaemp-
Heliotrope	Gerbera	Coleus	Perennial	feri)
Morning	Geum	Fuchsia	phlox	Meconopsis
glory	Gladiolus	Gloxinia	Portulaca	
Pelargonium	Gypsophila	Hydrangea	Rose	
Peony	Hollyhock	(pink)	Salvia	
Poppy,	Impatiens	Iris	Schizanthus	
Iceland	Lavender	(bearded)	Verbena	
Sweet pea	Lilies	Marigold		
Sweet	(madonna	Narcissus		
William	and regal)	Nasturtium		
	Lobelia	Nicotiana		
	Mignonette	Pansy		
	Petunia	Poinsettia		
	Red-hot-	Primrose		
	poker	Primula		
	Scabious	Stock		
	Snapdragon	Tulip		
	Spring	Violet		
	gentian			
	Sunflower			
	Wallflower			
	Zinnia			

SHRUBS AND TREES

Very sensitive pH6·5–8·0	*Sensitive* pH6·0–7·5	*Tolerant* pH5·5–7·0	*Very tolerant* pH0·0–0·0	*Acid-lovers* pH0·0–0·0
Abele	Cherry	Apple	Arbutus	Andromeda
Acacia	Cistus	Pear	unedo	(pieris)
Acer	(rock rose)	Privet	(strawberry	Azalea
(maple)	Daphne	Rose	tree)	Camellia
Berberis	Forsythia		Birch	Heath and
(barberry)	Fraxinus		Boronia	Heather
Buddleia	(ash)		Ceanothus	Hydrangea
Clematis	Genista		Comptonia	Ledum
Cotoneaster	Hamamelis		Corylopsis	Liquid-
Deutzia	mollis		Eucalyptus	ambar
Escallonia	(witch-hazel)		Gaultheria	Most conifers
Euonymus	Jasmine		(winter-	Pernettya
Hibiscus	Laurel		green)	Phyllodoce
(rose-	Mulberry		Grevillea	Pin oak
mallow)	Peach		Juniper	Rhododen-
Hypericum	Poplar		(common)	dron
(St John's	Prunus		Kalmia	Vaccinium
wort)	(plum,		(American	(bilberry)
Ivy	cherry, etc)		laurel)	Zenobia
(variegated)	Rhus		Leptospernum	
Japonica	Ribes		Leucothoe	
Kerria	(currant)		Lindera	
Laburnum	Senecio		Magnolia	
Lonicera	Syringa		Photinia	
(Honey-	(lilac)		Potentilla	
suckle)	Veronica		(cinquefoil)	
Philadelphus	Vibernum		Rosemary	
(mock-	Vitis (vine)		Styrax (storax)	
orange)	Willow			
Prunus				
(ornamental)				
Pyracanth				
(firethorn)				
Spiraea				
Weigelia				
(diervilla or				
bush				
honeysuckle)				

K

grow on moderately acid soils, but the ash and poplar prefer less acid soils.

LIMING MATERIALS

There are three main forms of liming materials:

		Relative neutralising value	Molecular weight
Ground chalk or limestone (calcium carbonate)	$CaCO_3$	100	100
Quicklime or burnt lime (calcium oxide)	CaO	178	56
Slaked or hydrated lime (builders' lime) (calcium hydrate)	$Ca(Oh)_2$	135	74

Unprocessed lump chalk can also be used if it is soft enough to break down under the influence of the weather. Quicklime or burnt lime is little used nowadays. It is caustic and liable to burn the hands and clothing. Slaked or hydrated lime (builder's lime) has had just enough water added to it to hydrate it and still leave it dry. When either form is exposed to the air it quickly returns to the carbonated form, calcium carbonate, absorbing carbon dioxide from the atmosphere.

Many gardeners, unfortunately, are gullible enough to pay absurdly high prices for 'garden' lime, often as much as ten times the ordinary commercial value of the product. Usually builder's lime (hydrated) is much cheaper, although even this is expensive for large-scale use. It is also rather unpleasant to use, being so finely pulverised that it gets into clothing and is blown about in the wind.

Since all three forms are essentially the same, their long-term effects are the same. Hydrated lime reacts with the soil more quickly and produces a higher pH at first than ground limestone. Ground chalk is also highly pulverised and quick-acting. If there is little time to alter the pH before sowing a crop, their fast action may be an advantage. But on light soils they may be quickly washed out of the soil: on these soils lime in coarser particles is desirable.

Ground limestones contain impurities such as sand or clay in varying proportions. Most limestones also contain some magnesium carbonate. And since both magnesium and calcium are essential plant nutrients and since both these carbonates neutralise soil acidity, magnesian limestone may be preferable to pure calcium carbonate. But the magnesian (dolomitic) limestones act slowly and need to be more finely ground than other forms.

Limestone is usually ground so that about 60 per cent of it will pass through a fine sieve which has 100 meshes to the inch or 10,000 holes per sq in. The fine material then reacts quickly with the soil, but the coarser particles provide a reserve of calcium. The coarser particles are especially useful on sandy soils in which finely ground materials are likely to be washed down rapidly into the lower soil layers.

Calcium is also supplied by superphosphate. Superphosphate contains almost 25 per cent calcium, but it does not neutralise soil acidity. It may be especially valuable for supplying calcium to such crops as potatoes without raising the soil pH.

Wood ashes can also be a useful source of lime. Hardwood ashes contain up to 40 per cent of lime, as well as potash and other nutrients. But these materials need to be lightly spread when dry, and raked into the topsoil; otherwise they become sticky or form a crust on the soil.

AMOUNTS TO APPLY

The pH test reveals whether a soil needs lime, but not how much lime to apply. Since most garden crops grow well at around pH6·5, recommendations are usually based on the amounts to apply in order to bring the soil pH up to pH6–6·5.

Soils are 'buffered' against changes in their acidity. If this were not so, a few pounds of lime would be enough to change the pH of a whole acre of soil. Clay soils and soils with much organic matter, such as fen or peat soils, are strongly buffered and resist changes in their pH. Light and sandy soils of coarse texture are weakly buffered. This means that far more lime has to be given in clay than in sandy soils to alter the soil reaction.

The 'reserve' or potential acidity of a soil consists of the hydrogen which is held on the surface of clay and humus particles. A sandy soil which contains little clay or humus is therefore easily neutralised, because it has no 'reserve' acidity.

The amount of lime to apply will depend on several factors:

1   the present pH of the soil;
2   the amounts of clay and organic matter in the soil (the more clay and humus there is in the soil, the more lime is needed to change the pH);
3   the kind of plants to be grown;
4   the purity and fineness of the liming material.

As a rough guide, the amount of lime needed to raise the pH of soil through one pH unit is:

Approximate amount of ground limestone or chalk needed to raise the topsoil by one unit of pH:

Sand and sandy loam	½lb per sq yd (1 ton per acre)
Average loam	1lb per sq yd (2 tons per acre)
Clay	1½lb per sq yd (3–3½ tons per acre)

Of burnt lime about half the above amounts are used; of hydrated lime (builder's lime) about three-quarters.

Dressings higher than 1½lb per sq yd are rarely needed, since few clay soils are extremely acid. But some gardeners who have heavy soils may use larger amounts of lime or chalk to improve soil tilth, and to provide a reserve of calcium.

Even so, the amounts required are fairly large: on an average soil about 1lb of limestone per sq yd is needed to raise the soil through one pH unit. This is probably a larger amount than most gardeners are used to applying.

As relatively small amounts are required to change the pH of sandy soils, there is some danger of over-liming them and of inducing trace-element deficiencies. On medium loam or clays, heavy liming causes no trouble. But on light acid soils, it is better to raise the pH only one division each year; or to give

frequent small dressings checking repeatedly on the pH. In practice, applying only about half the lime requirement to sandy soils
gives almost as good results as applying the full amount.

The figures given in the table are only a general guide. The
advice of local experts should be sought wherever possible.

Liming a soil is a long-term process. Once a soil has been
well limed, it should not need an equally heavy dressing for some
years. In farm practice, six to eight years may elapse before re-
liming. On sandy soils in high rainfall districts, on the other hand,
calcium may be leached from the soil at such a rate that more
frequent dressings are needed.

TIME OF APPLICATION

Hydrated lime is quicker in action than ground limestone, being
more powdery and more readily soluble. Finely ground chalk
and limestone take about six months to have their full effect on
pH, and the coarser limestone grades take about a year or even
longer. Even hydrated lime that has been well mixed with the
soil, probably takes two or three months to neutralise the acidity
of a soil which contains much clay and humus. This means that
all forms of lime are best applied about six months before sowing
a crop. In particular, burnt lime or quicklime should be applied
about six months before sowing, otherwise the caustic properties
may damage the germinating seeds. Response to lime runs well
ahead of pH change, for as plant roots proliferate and come into
contact with particles of lime, they encounter minute zones in
which nutrients have been made soluble by the presence of the
lime.

In general it is best to dig in lime in the autumn. The only
exception to this rule is in the case of hydrated lime on coarse
sandy soil, when winter rain might wash the fine particles into
the lower soil layers. Apart from this case, chalk, ground limestone and hydrated lime can be applied at any time of the year.
But for vegetables such as peas and beans, cauliflower and beet,
onions and lettuce, it is as well to apply lime some six months
in advance of seeding so that it can have its full effect on pH.

When potatoes are grown, lime should not be given. Lime makes conditions more favourable for the organisms which produce scab. This is a source of difficulty in the vegetable garden, for the majority of other vegetables grow best at pH6–6·5. It is best to lime after the potato crop, and to move the potatoes the next year to a plot which has not been recently limed. In most soils scab does not occur below pH5·5.

METHOD OF APPLICATION

Lime needs to be well mixed with the soil. On medium and heavy soils it should not be just scattered on the surface, as is often done. The lime should be evenly distributed throughout the topsoil. In digging, lime should be scattered so that some will be near the subsoil, and some incorporated at all depths of the topsoil. This will ensure that no pockets of acidity are left, and that acidity is rapidly corrected.

Lime should not be mixed with ammonium salts such as sulphate of ammonia, or nitrogen will be lost as ammonia gas. The same applies to mixing lime and animal manures outside the soil. This means that manure and lime should not be spread on the surface of the ground at the same time.

Lime should be applied in advance of potassium fertilisers, for the lime puts calcium ions on the soil colloids and these can then be readily displaced by potassium ions.

MAKING SOIL MORE ACID

It is sometimes desirable to make a soil more acid in order to grow such plants as rhododendrons and azaleas. If there is free lime in the soil, the soil should be removed to a depth of some 18in and replaced by a woodland soil or by peat. When peat and leaf-mould decay, the soil becomes more acid. Mixtures of one part soil to one part acid peat (peat moss) are suitable for hydrangeas. Azaleas may be grown in a soil which is mostly peat, provided they receive manure or fertiliser as well.

If the soil does not contain free lime, powdered sulphur, or ferrous sulphate, or aluminium sulphate can be added to acidify

it. Aluminium sulphate (alum) is used on hydrangeas since the
flower pigment changes from pink to blue when excess aluminium is absorbed. But about seven times as much aluminium
sulphate as sulphur is required to acidify the soil by the same
amount.

Powdered sulphur is the cheapest material, but ferrous sulphate
is more satisfactory, since it may also provide iron. About 4oz
per sq yd of either substance is required.

Aluminium sulphate and iron sulphate take about fourteen
days to become effective. Powdered sulphur takes from three to
six months. Sulphur is best applied in spring. Soils to be treated
should be well drained, otherwise hydrogen sulphide is produced.

Soil acidity can be maintained by using acid fertilisers such as
sulphate of ammonia. Lime of course should not be applied, nor
bone-meal, wood ashes, nor sand containing limestone; nor
should hard tap-water be used.

When the lime content of the soil is too great for azaleas and
other flowering shrubs, as shown by yellowing of the foliage
and by stunted growth, iron can be supplied by iron chelates
such as 'Sequestrene'. In these chelated compounds the iron is in
such a form that it does not become fixed and unusable in chalk
soils. Calcifuges are more tolerant of lime when the soil contains
a good supply of organic matter, for organic matter holds iron
and manganese in compounds which are to some extent assimilable
even in chalk or limestone.

CHAPTER 8

THE TRACE ELEMENTS

Askine why this flower doth show
So yellow-green and sickly too
(Herrick)

Research on plant nutrition has shown that in addition to the major nutrients – nitrogen, phosphorus, potassium, calcium, magnesium and sulphur – plants also require other mineral elements for their normal healthy growth. These elements are required in minute quantities or traces and are therefore known as trace elements. They include iron, manganese, copper, zinc, boron and molybdenum. These metallic elements have many functions in plant chemistry. Chiefly they serve as activators of the enzymes which speed up chemical reactions. Over 200 plant enzymes are known to be influenced by mineral elements.

Fertilisers usually contain nitrogen, phosphorus and potassium only and are therefore often referred to as NPK fertilisers. Nitrogen, phosphorus and potassium are indeed required in greater amounts than the other essential nutrients and they are known to be deficient in many soils, although in recent years unnecessarily large amounts of potassium have been used. But the other nine minerals may also be deficient. There is evidence that trace-element deficiencies are becoming more common. This is one result of the change from animal manures to inorganic fertilisers. For good farmyard manure or compost contains useful amounts of all the essential elements, whereas most inorganic fertilisers do not.

A shortage of one or more trace elements results usually in

recognisable visual symptoms, making the leaves pale or mottled or causing death of the growing points. But it is also possible that latent deficiencies may reduce the growth and vigour of plants without giving rise to distinctive symptoms. Expert opinion tends to be against adding trace elements to fertilisers as an 'insurance policy', unless a deficiency is definitely known to exist; for an excess of trace elements is harmful, and they are required in such small quantities – in the case of molybdenum only about 1oz per acre – that it is very easy to give too much and difficult to ensure even distribution. Nevertheless, in those parts of the world in which trace deficiencies are known to be common, such as the eastern Australian states, trace elements are added to garden fertilisers as a matter of routine.

TRACE-ELEMENT TOXICITIES

Manganese is one trace element which is sometimes present in excess. Manganese toxicity is fairly common in new greenhouse soils which have been sterilised at high temperatures. Sterilisation releases soil manganese and makes it available to plants in large amounts. Susceptible plants which are damaged by high soil manganese include lettuce and chrysanthemums.

In the same way, the other trace elements can also be present in such high amounts that growth is reduced.

THE WORLD-WIDE DISTRIBUTION OF DEFICIENCIES

There is now a growing body of knowledge about the nutrient needs of different kinds of plant and also of the kinds of soil which are likely to be deficient in trace elements. It is therefore possible to make some intelligent guesses as to why certain plants fail to flourish in particular areas – although it is easy to confuse the effects of insect damage, spray and herbicide damage, and bad weather with deficiency symptoms.

It is worth emphasising that the world's soils are not all naturally fertile and not necessarily adapted to the kinds of plant that men wish to grow. Plants have evolved over the long ages of geological time to suit certain conditions of soil and climate. Australian native plants, for instance, have very low phosphate requirements because Australian soils have a very low phosphate content. Frequently native plants are healthy while imported plants may suffer from malnutrition. Many trees and flowers are transported from one continent to another where soil conditions may be very different; few horticultural crops are natives of the soil in which they grow, and intensive cultivation and improved varieties everywhere make increased demands on the soil's stock of all the mineral nutrients.

The trace elements may be deficient either because the original parent materials of soil were deficient or because the soil's stock of trace elements has been exhausted by intensive cropping without replacement. Deficiencies are worldwide and not confined to developed areas. Thus deficiencies of copper, boron and manganese are common in parts of Britain and Northern Europe. In the USA copper, zinc, boron and manganese affect many regions, including the fruit-producing areas of Florida and California. In many parts of the world, as a result of the monoculture of demanding crops such as coffee, soils become deficient in zinc and magnesium. In Malaya iron and manganese deficiencies occur on rubber plantations, and in Ceylon copper is deficient in tea plantations. In South Africa copper, zinc and manganese are deficient in some of the fruit-growing areas of the Cape. And in Australia the acute deficiencies of zinc, copper and molybdenum have been diagnosed and corrected only in recent years.

Although the same elements are required by all plants, some species need more of certain elements than others, and some species are less damaged by excess amounts of trace elements than others. There are also varietal differences within species. Whether a plant is sensitive to lack of a trace element in the soil, depends partly on how much it requires of the element and partly on how effective its roots are in extracting the element from the soil. Young plants and newly transplanted specimens are vulnerable because they have not had time to fill the soil with their roots.

Plants need *iron* in greater amounts than the other trace elements. Iron is abundant in many soils, giving them their red and brown hues. But chalk and limestone soils may contain little iron in usable form. Fruit-trees and vines growing in such soils frequently suffer from iron deficiency.

Iron is required for the manufacture of the green chlorophyll. Iron deficiency therefore leads to chlorosis – that is, failure to produce the normal green chlorophyll – new leaves becoming a pale yellow and developing pale areas between the veins; first the leaf turns pale, then there is a yellowing between the veins and finally the entire leaf turns yellow or even white, but it does not fall or die.

Iron deficiency in a sweet cherry leaf

Available iron is usually abundant in acid soils: in fact, in acid soils too much iron may be present, especially if the soil is poorly drained. Deficiencies tend to be confined to trace and bush fruits growing on chalk or limestone or on soil which has been heavily limed. Ornamental plants such as azaleas, magnolias, camellias and hydrangeas, and many conifers, also suffer from iron starvation under these conditions.

Manganese deficiency is widespread throughout the world. In Europe it is probably the most common trace-element deficiency, affecting many kinds of horticultural crops. It occurs mainly on three kinds of soil: on black peaty soils, on acid sandy soils, and on calcareous clays. Thus in Britain it occurs on the East Anglian fens and on the leached sands of the Lancashire plain. Some badly drained clays are also deficient.

The amount of available manganese in soils varies a great deal, and the amounts taken up by plants are also extremely variable, depending on the amount in the soil and on its state in the soil. Hence, plants suffer from both deficiency and excess of manganese.

Deficiency symptoms in some ways resemble those of iron. The leaf veins remain green and the areas between the veins become yellow. In severe cases the entire leaf turns yellow. Unlike iron, manganese deficiency also causes brownish dead spots parallel to the veins. The visible effects are, however, diverse. In potatoes dead spots occur along the veins of young leaves. In other plants the older leaves are first affected.

Copper, which is needed in only very small amounts, tends to be lacking in light peaty soils, and in some sands. Deficiencies are common on black organic soils derived from chalk downland, and on reclaimed heaths. Heavy fertilising with nitrogen fertiliser may induce copper deficiency in the tips of shoots. Farmyard manure, on the other hand, usually contains an adequate supply of copper.

The distinctive signs of copper deficiency are that the youngest leaves turn yellow and become twisted and curled. Deficiency is common in fruit-trees where it results in 'summer dieback' of apples and pears; leaf tips die, the leaf margins scorch, then the whole shoot dies back. The bark is rough and may develop dead areas.

It has been noticed for many years that spraying with the fungicide Bordeaux mixture, which contains copper, sometimes result in an increase in the growth and vigour of plants. If copper deficiency is suspected, the easiest test is to spray with Bordeaux mixture and note the results.

Zinc deficiency is most prevalent in those climates where there is much bright sunlight. It is important in citrus orchards in the USA, South Africa and Australia. In Britain it has been reported in apple orchards on light soils. Like other trace-element deficiencies, it tends to occur on organic peat soils and on neutral or alkaline soils.

In fruit-trees the symptoms are of 'little leaf': clusters of small yellowish leaves growing at the ends of twigs, and these small leaves having a rosette appearance. In citrus trees the symptoms are yellow mottling of the leaves and of the young terminal leaflets.

No less than sixteen functions have been ascribed to *boron* in the plant. It is concerned with flowering and fruiting, with the uptake and movement of calcium and with the movement of sugars and starches within the plant. Plants such as turnips, swedes and beets, which store quantities of starch in their roots, are some of the first to show the characteristic 'heart-rot', the roots developing brown dead areas or in severe cases becoming hollow in the centre. Above the ground, boron deficiency like calcium deficiency results in death and blackening of the growing points.

It is prevalent on sandy soils in dry summers, particularly on soils that have been limed. It is of such common occurrence in Europe that susceptible root crops are often dressed with a small quantity of borax as a matter of routine. Brassica crops, especially cauliflower, are also susceptible, showing brown lesions within the stems and browning of the curds.

Molybdenum is required only in minute quantities: 1oz per acre is an ample dressing which need not be repeated for some years. It was the latest of the trace elements to be discovered. In 1942 experiments on some hills of unexplained infertility in South Australia revealed that molybdenum was the missing element.

In its absence clovers would not grow, as it is needed by the root-nodule bacteria which fix nitrogen. Subsequently it has also been shown to be essential for the reduction of nitrate nitrogen within the plant. Many of the soils of eastern Australia are deficient in

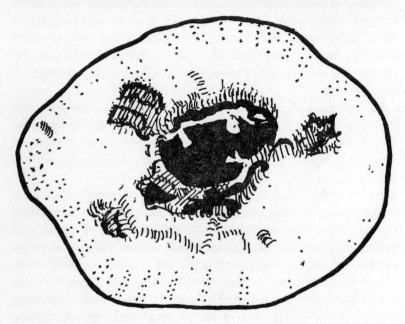

Cross section of turnip root showing heart-rot due to boron deficiency

molybdenum, and in some areas dramatic conversion of scrub to productive farmland became possible.

In Britain a deficiency of molybdenum is fairly common in horticultural crops such as cauliflowers and lettuce on the leached sands of the North West. Unlike the other trace elements, molybdenum becomes less available in acid soils and can often be released by liming. In general those crops which need much lime, as legumes and brassicas, have also a high need for molybdenum.

The deficiency may appear as a yellow-green mottling of the leaves, following by marginal wilting. Translucent areas develop close to the midribs and break into holes. In 'whiptail' of cauliflowers the leaf blade is narrow, giving the stalk the appearance of a whip.

Since molybdenum is required in such small amounts, but may be taken up in harmfully large amounts if it is plentiful in the soil, it is better to attempt to correct deficiencies by liming rather

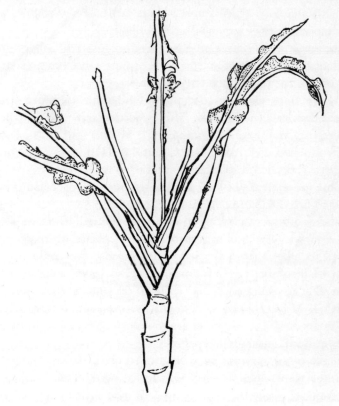

Molybdenum deficiency. 'Whiptail' in cauliflower

than by giving dressings or sprayings of molybdenum unless, as in the Antipodes, molybdenum is known to be absent from the soil.

AVAILABILITY OF THE TRACE ELEMENTS
The supply of trace elements depends not only on the amounts

occurring in the soil but also on the form in which they are present, which in turn depends on pH, organic-matter content, aeration and climate. Like other mineral nutrients, the trace elements may be present in solution or be adsorbed on clay and humus, or they may be contained in compounds of varying degrees of solubility. In solution they are readily available, as exchangeable ions on clay and humus rather less available, while in compounds they are usually unavailable.

The amounts of trace elements therefore, as of all other mineral nutrients, depend not only on the absolute amounts present but also on the form in which they occur.

All the trace elements except molybdenum are more soluble in acid than in alkaline soils. This is particularly true of iron and manganese. Iron and manganese exist in acid soils in the soluble bivalent form, Fe^{++} and Mn^{++}, but in alkaline soils in higher valences (bonding capacities), eg Fe^{+++} and Mn^{++++}. As soils become more alkaline, iron and manganese are increasingly oxidised to unavailable oxides and hydroxides.

Where soils are waterlogged or poorly aerated, iron compounds are reduced. The soil micro-organisms, short of oxygen, are forced to take it from the iron compounds, thus reducing iron from its insoluble ferric form (eg Fe_2O_3) to its soluble ferrous form (FeO). Manganese is reduced in much the same way $(MnO_2 \rightarrow Mn_2O_3 \rightarrow MnO)$. Thus in poorly aerated acid soils excess quantities of manganese are in solution, accumulate in plant roots and kill susceptible species.

At the other extreme, in well-aerated chalk or limestone soils, calcifuge plants such as rhododendrons, which have a large iron requirement, show the typical signs of iron deficiency, the young leaves being pale and chlorotic. Hydrangeas also show pale areas between the leaf veins under these conditions.

THE EFFECT OF pH ON AVAILABILITY

Of the other micronutrients, zinc, copper and boron are also less available at higher pH. Zinc is readily available below pH5·5, but increasingly less available above this level. Copper is held most tightly at pH7–8, less at pH6 and increasingly less as the soil becomes more acid. It is held in particularly insoluble form in organic compounds, and therefore tends to be deficient in peat or muck soils. Soluble boron is present mostly in the organic matter of the topsoil, from which it is released by micro-organisms. Its availability decreases above pH7. The functions of boron are closely related to those of calcium, and the two elements need to be in balance. Heavy dressings of lime often lead to boron deficiency, especially on light sandy soils. This is especially likely to occur in hot dry summers. When the topsoil is dry and nutrient uptake from the surface layers is restricted, plants are unable to take up sufficient boron from the lower soil horizons.

Soil pH, which strongly influences the availability of the trace elements, is subject to seasonal fluctuations, frequently varying by as much as a whole pH unit. The general effect is for pH to increase as the soil dries out. There is thus a general tendency for trace-element deficiencies to occur in hot dry summers.

Molybdenum differs from the other trace elements in that it becomes more available as pH increases. It is held in exchangeable form in clay minerals, and is also slowly released from organic matter. In acid soils it is bound to hydrous iron and aluminium oxides and is unavailable. Liming soils release molybdenum, so that molybdenum fertilisation is likely to be necessary only where soils do not contain the 1–2ppm of the element which are normally present. In fact, it is sometimes claimed that the beneficial effect of liming may be merely to release sufficient molybdenum.

Plants absorb large quantities of molybdenum. Up to 300ppm may be present in plant tissues, if it is available in the soil, although less than 1ppm is adequate for normal growth. A high uptake of molybdenum does not appear to have an adverse effect on the plants. But if animals consume such plants, their copper metabolism is disturbed. In animal nutrition there has to be a balance in the uptake of copper and molybdenum.

KINDS OF SOIL LIKELY TO BE DEFICIENT

Certain kinds of soil frequently lack trace elements: leached

L

sands, peats and calcareous soils. Leached sands tend to be poorly supplied with all the nutrient elements. Peats and organic soils tend to lock up the metallic trace elements, especially copper, in unavailable forms. Chalk and limestone soils, being alkaline, tend to make all the trace elements unavailable (except molybdenum).

The following trace-element deficiencies are common on these types of soil:

Leached sands	Organic soils and fen peats	Chalk and limestone
Manganese, zinc	Copper	Iron
	Manganese	Manganese
Boron, copper	Zinc	Boron, copper
Molybdenum		

VISUAL SIGNS OF TRACE-ELEMENT DEFICIENCIES

Deficiencies of trace elements do not always result in unambiguous visual symptoms. A shortage of one or more of the essential elements may be shown in a number of ways: total failure of seeds to germinate, abnormal leaf symptoms, stunted growth or poor quality of fruits and flowers. Moreover, deficiencies are relative and depend upon the balance of nutrients. Iron deficiency, for example, may be induced by the presence of large amounts of manganese, zinc and other metals.

But even so, it is possible to diagnose nutrient deficiencies fairly reliably from close observation of certain visual signs. In the case of some elements such as boron the signs are specific and unlikely to be mistaken for what they are not; in the case of other elements, particularly manganese, the symptoms are not so clear-cut and take different forms in different plants. In all cases it is desirable to cross-check on other species known to be susceptible, so-called 'indicator' plants, and to consider any other kinds of available evidence.

As a further caveat it should again be emphasised that very similar kinds of damage can be caused by frost, drought and waterlogging, and by insect pests and plant diseases, and that damage by these agents is probably more common than that caused by nutrient deficiencies. Bearing this in mind, suspected trace-element deficiencies can be identified by the logical elimination of alternatives.

Deficiencies of the trace elements, except molybdenum and zinc, and with the partial exception of manganese, first affect the young leaves rather than the entire plant; whereas deficiencies of the major elements, nitrogen, phosphorus, potassium and magnesium either affect the entire plant or first affect the older or lower leaves. The reason for this is that elements, such as potassium, which are mobile within the plant, are translocated to meet the needs of the new growth, whereas elements which are immobile, such as calcium and many of the trace elements, cannot be so translocated.

	Entire plant or older or lower leaves mostly affected	New leaves affected first
Possible deficiencies	Nitrogen, phosphorus, potassium, magnesium Molybdenum, zinc (manganese)	Calcium, sulphur Iron (manganese), copper, boron

Assuming that the younger leaves are affected, a further distinction can be made, depending on the condition of the young leaves of the terminal buds:

	Terminal bud dies, after distortion of young leaves	Terminal bud remains alive. Wilting or chlorosis of younger or bud leaves
Possible deficiencies	Calcium, boron (copper)	(Copper), manganese, sulphur, iron

Having limited the possibilities to this extent, identification is best made by reference to the specific deficiency symptoms of each element:

Nitrogen   Probably the most common of all deficiencies. Effects involve the whole plant, with drying or browning of the lower leaves. Plant turns pale light green. Reddish tints appear in the leaves later in the season. Growth is thin and shrunken

Phosphorus	Effects involve the whole plant, the lower leaves drying to greenish-brown. Leaf colour is a dull bluish-green, often developing purple tints
Potassium	Beginning on the older leaves: scorching of the leaf margins and brown spots developing near the leaf margins which roll inwards
Magnesium	Beginning on the older leaves: mottling or chlorosis of the leaves, leading to defoliation
Zinc	Yellow mottling of leaves and rosetting of young terminal leaflets. Small leaves
Molybdenum	Beginning on the older leaves: intervenal yellow-green mottling of leaves, translucent areas on leaves, breaking into holes. Failure of lamina to develop
Calcium	Newer or bud leaves affected. Young leaves of terminal buds characteristically hooked downwards, dying back of leaf tips and margins. Death and blackening of stem apex
Boron	Terminal leaves twisted. Death of terminal buds. In root crops, hollow and browned areas in centre of roots
Copper	Terminal buds remain alive. Young leaves are twisted and wilted. Little spotting or chlorosis. Shoot dieback in pome fruits
Manganese	Terminal buds remain alive. Young leaves are not wilted, but older leaves show yellow-green intervenal chlorosis, the smallest veins remaining green, giving a checkered appearance. Spots of dead tissue over the leaf
Iron	Young leaves pale and chlorotic, even bleached; the principal and often minor veins stay green. Dead spots not usually present
Sulphur	Young leaves light green. Dead spots not present. (This deficiency does not occur in industrial areas.)

In many varieties of fruits and vegetables the deficiency symptoms are distinct enough to permit differential diagnosis, but in some species they may not be so clear, and it is therefore desirable to confirm symptoms on other kinds of plant growing in the same soil. For instance, if in the same garden swedes show symptoms of 'heart-rot', cauliflowers of 'hollow-stem' and apples of 'cork', boron deficiency can be diagnosed with some confidence. Certain plants are known to be good indicators of particular deficiencies: not only are these indicator plants sensitive to deficiencies but they show them in unambiguous form. In temperate climates some of the best indicator plants are those to be found growing in most gardens: brassicas, especially the cauliflower, potatoes and apple trees.

Possible indicator plants are:

Element	Indicator plant	Symptoms
Nitrogen	Cauliflower, cabbage, apple, blackcurrant	Stunted growth, pale green leaves developing yellow and orange tints
Phosphorus	Rape, kale	Dull purple tints on leaves
	Swede, turnip	Premature defoliation
	Apple, gooseberry	Poor growth
	Tomato	Tomato shows purpling on undersides of leaves
Potassium	Potato, cauliflower, broad bean, runner bean, gooseberry, apple	Leaf margins scorched
Calcium	Cauliflower, cabbage	In the brassicas a narrow white band appears on leaf margins
Magnesium	Cauliflower, potato	In cauliflower, chlorosis of older leaves. In potato, browning of centre and margins of leaves
	Gooseberry, blackcurrant	In gooseberry, red marginal bands. In blackcurrant, leaf centres are purple
	Apple	In apples, intervenal brown scorch on older leaves of terminal shoots, followed by early defoliation
Sulphur	Cabbage, onion	Leaves pale green to yellow. Appears first on new growth

Element	Indicator plant	Symptoms	Other susceptible plants
Iron	Cauliflower, cabbage, apple, raspberry	Young leaves of terminal shoots are chlorotic and may be bleached	Plum, pear, blackcurrant, gooseberry, ornamental calcifuges
Manganese	Beet, potato, apple, cherry	Leaves show mottled intervenal chlorosis. In potato, there are also brown spots along leaf veins. Chlorosis does begin at tip, as for iron	Brassicas, pea, bean, petunia, stock, geranium, strawberry, raspberry
Copper	Tomato	In tomato, curling or twisting of leaves	Lettuce, onion, spinach, carrot, beet, cabbage
	Apple, pear	In fruit-trees, death of leaf tips, marginal scorch, dieback of shoots and witches'-broom habit. Splits in bark, gum exuded	
Boron	Swede, turnip, cauliflower	In cauliflower, the stem is hollow and discoloured internally. 'Heart-rot' of swedes and turnips	Celery, asparagus, radish, sunflower, aster
	Apple	In apples, small misshapen fruit, internal and external 'cork'	
	Broad bean	In broad bean, terminal bud blackens and dies back	

Element	Indicator plant	Symptoms	Other susceptible plants
Zinc	Citrus	In citrus, yellow intervenal mottling of leaves	Green bean, grape, maize
	Apple	In apple, 'little leaf' or rosette	
Molybdenum	Cauliflower	In cauliflower, 'whiptail'. Failure to head	Citrus, legumes
	Lettuce	In lettuce, chlorosis followed by death of leaf margins	

SPRAYING AS A MEANS OF DIAGNOSIS

Since plants can take in nutrients through their leaves as well as through their roots, uncertainties in visual diagnosis can some- times be resolved by spraying or watering nutrient solutions on the leaves. When plants are young, response to the spraying may be seen after seven to ten days, since nutrients, with the exception of iron, are quickly used. Suitable solutions per 2gal of water are:

Manganese	Manganous sulphate	2oz
Boron	Borax or sodium tetraborate	2oz
Copper	Cuprous oxide or copper oxychloride (or Bor- deaux powder)	½oz
Zinc	Zinc sulphate	½oz
Molybdenum	Sodium molybdate	⅓oz
Iron	Iron chelates	
	Iron – EDHPA	½oz
	(Sequestrene 138 – iron)	

The solution is watered or sprayed on a sample of plants, leaving the rest untreated as controls. A detergent 'wetter' needs to be added so that the solution does not run off the leaves. It is also as well to add a little hydrated lime to copper, manganese and zinc sprays to avoid burning the leaves, or to use weaker solu- tions.

Sulphate of iron, even in dilute solution, tends to damage the leaves, and it has therefore not been included in the above list. Moreover, iron is so immobile in the plant that iron deficiency is not influenced readily by leaf-spraying.

The same method can of course be used where deficiencies of the major nutrients are suspected. About 4oz per 2gal of compounds such as superphosphate, sulphate of potash, Epsom salts, etc may be used. There is little response to the Epsom salts (magnesium) treatment, however, unless the spraying is repeated three or four times at intervals of fourteen days.

CORRECTIVE MEASURES

Care must be taken not to apply toxic amounts of trace elements. Since fertiliser dressings are so small, the trace elements are usually mixed with sand or other fertilisers or sprayed on plants in solution.

Soil applications of boron are commonly in the form of borax (sodium borate), which contains 11 per cent boron. Higher grade materials such as solubor contain 20 per cent boron. Rates of application average about 1oz per 15sq yd (20lb an acre) and the amount should be broadcast mixed with fine sand or with another fertiliser. Foliar sprayings with a 0·3 per cent borax solution (1oz per 2gal) are effective on fruit-trees, but most other plants need to be sprayed a number of times in the course of the growing season, since boron is immobile in the plant.

Manganese can be sprayed on to plants, using a 0·3 per cent solution (approximately 1oz per 2gal of water) of manganese sulphate. One such spraying may be sufficient to correct deficiencies, but better results have been obtained by spraying a more dilute (0·1 per cent) solution once every three weeks. Soil applications to alkaline soils are ineffective since the manganese is quickly converted to unavailable forms. In peat soils soil applications of 1oz per 10sq yd are effective.

Copper is supplied in soil applications of copper sulphate at rates of 1oz to 10–15sq yd mixed with sand or other fertilisers. Peat soils require heavy dressings. Only light dressings should be given on sandy soils so that toxic levels will not be built up.

Zinc deficiency is usually corrected by spraying a 0·2 per cent solution of zinc sulphate. Injection into trees and zinc-coated nails driven into tree-trunks have also been used. Soil applications of zinc sulphate at about 1oz per 15sq yd (30lb an acre) have not always been successful.

Molybdenum deficiency is best tackled by liming the soil if it is acid. Because of the tiny amounts of molybdenum required, normally 2oz per acre, molybdenum is best applied by foliar spraying of young plants or by spraying seeds before they are planted, using a 0·05 per cent solution of sodium molybdate.

Iron deficiency is difficult and expensive to correct. It cannot be corrected on the alkaline soils on which it is most likely to occur, by soil application of iron salts, because the soil 'fixes' the iron. And sprayings with ferrous sulphate damage leaves and are usually ineffective. The most helpful remedy is chelated iron, either sprayed or watered in to the soil. Of the iron chelates, iron-EDHPA (sequestrene 138-iron) has proved to be the most effective. The amount of chelate required depends upon the size of the plant or tree. Small plants need to be watered with 2gal per sq yd of 0·1 per cent solution (1oz to 6gal of water). Larger trees require 3–4oz per tree, well watered in over the ground area covered by the branches. Iron chelates are so expensive, however, that it is doubtless more sensible not to attempt to grow fruit on chalk.

A natural chelate can be made by spraying ½oz of sulphate of iron over a bushel of peat. This product can then be dug into beds intended for susceptible ornamental plants.

CHAPTER 9

COMPOSTS – LIQUID
AND FOLIAR FEEDING

For beside the common way and road of reception
by the root, there may be a refection and imbibition
from without: for gentle showrs refresh plants,
though they enter not their roots.

(Sir Thomas Browne)

SEED AND POTTING COMPOSTS

When seedlings and cuttings are grown in pots, trays and containers, ordinary soils are unsuitable. Ordinary soil is too heavy,
too little aerated, and does not hold enough moisture. On drying,
it tends to shrink away from the sides of containers, so that when
it is watered, the water runs down the sides and out of the drainage
holes without wetting the soil.

Seed and potting composts have to be well aerated and retentive of moisture, yet at the same time dense enough to hold
seedlings firmly in place. They need to provide adequate nutrients
for the young plant, without the high levels of salinity which
might damage germinating seeds. And they need to be sterile –
that is, free from insects, nematodes and harmful bacteria and
fungi, particularly the fungi which cause damping-off in seed
beds.

These requirements have traditionally been met by mixtures of
sterilised loam, sand and peat, supplemented by appropriate lime
and fertiliser. The well-known John Innes composts are of this
type. As good loam has become scarce, loamless composts have
been developed consisting of sand and peat only. These loamless

composts, since they do not contain the nutrients supplied by the loam, need to be fortified with more elaborate fertiliser supplements. They are more liable to become waterlogged than loam mixes, since they use a finer sand which does not drain as readily as the coarser sand used in loam composts. On the other hand, peat and sand are usually sterile, and it is therefore possible to dispense with the difficult process of steam or chemical sterilisation.

MATERIALS

Sand Sand varies in its mineral constituents, in the size of its grains and in pH. Builder's river-washed quartz sands, which are free from clay and silt, are generally suitable. Sand taken from sea beaches or from dunes near the sea has too high a salt content to be usable.

For the John Innes type of loam compost, the sand should be coarse, having most of its particles $\frac{1}{8}-\frac{1}{10}$ in in size.

For loamless composts the sand needs to be finer and more uniform in texture, in order to bind the compost into a close mixture from which the constituents will not separate out. The type of sand used by builders for plastering or for mortar is often satisfactory.

Sands may be examined under a magnifying glass for impurities; rubbed between the fingers to see if they ball too easily; or shaken into water in a glass jar to see if they contain silt or clay. After being shaken, sand sinks quickly to the bottom of the jar, but clay takes over an hour to settle and leaves the water muddy and cloudy.

Peat For loam composts, peat should be of the brown, fibrous, granulated type. Fine black peats of sooty texture are unsuitable since they do not bind with the other ingredients and are difficult to wet when they dry out. Texture and stage of decomposition are more important than the original matter, whether sedge or moss. The particles should be $\frac{1}{8}-\frac{3}{8}$in in size. If necessary, the peat should be shredded through a $\frac{3}{8}$in riddle. The pH of the peat should be between pH4 and 5.

A finer grade of peat of particle size $\frac{1}{4}$in downwards is used for loamless composts. This fine peat needs to be broken apart and moistened before being mixed with sand, and it should not be allowed to dry out at any stage.

Loam The best loam for composts is a medium loam, which contains just enough clay to produce a ribbon of soil when smeared between the fingers, without being sticky or plastic. Sandy soil, heavy clay and chalky soils are unsuitable. A supply of organic matter in the loam is ensured by cutting turves from pasture, and stacking them grass side down in a heap about 6ft in diameter. The moist turves are stacked in late spring, leaving gaps in the heap for aeration. Decomposition is speeded if layers of turf are alternated with thin layers of stable manure.

If the soil of the turves is acid, it should be limed to pH6·2 and should not be used if it is below pH5·5. Turves which have been waterlogged or which contain a mat of undecomposed organic matter are also unsuitable, since when they are heated, large and toxic quantities of manganese are released.

The grass tops and roots decompose in about six months in temperate climates, faster in hot climates. The finished product, which should be covered if it is to be kept over winter, supplies most of the nutrients required by young seedlings except phosphorus, calcium and magnesium, which are added to the mix before seeding.

Other materials include vermiculite and perlite. Expanded vermiculite is a magnesium-aluminium-iron silicate, light in weight, neutral in reaction and able to absorb much water. It has some cation-exchange capacity and can supply potash and magnesium. It is available in various particle sizes, seed composts being of the finer grades, of particle size 1mm. If pressed or compacted when wet it loses its porous structure, and its physical properties are less satisfactory than those of sand.

STERILISATION

The object of soil sterilisation is to kill weed seeds, insects, slugs and nematodes, plant viruses, harmful bacteria and fungi. Loam should be sterilised separately before being mixed into composts.

Heat treatment is more efficacious than chemical methods, but if the soil is treated at too high a temperature for too long, the product is an unsuitable medium for the more delicate seedlings.

If steam is used and the loam heated to 100° C, an excess of ammonium is released, and manganese is also likely to become available in toxic amounts. To some extent the effects of the manganese are counteracted by adding superphosphate to the compost, but once manganese has been released, liming the compost is not a corrective. Crops susceptible to manganese toxicity include lettuce, chrysanthemums and antirrhinums.

Although steaming is the most convenient means of heat treatment, it is in fact preferable to use lower temperatures, since steam, as well as releasing too much ammonium and manganese, kills some of the beneficial organisms along with the harmful ones. Nearly all harmful organisms are killed at 70° or 80° C, and the damping-off fungi and nematodes at 60° C.

Thus it is unnecessary to heat soil to 100° C, as most pathogenic organisms will be destroyed at 70° C (approx 160° F).

Temperatures at which soil organisms are killed, ie when heated for thirty minutes in moist conditions

80° C	Most weed seeds
70° C	Soil insects, nitrifying bacteria, all harmful bacteria, most viruses
60° C	Worms, slugs, fusarium wilt, botrytis mould
50° C	Nematodes, damping-off fungi

It is, however, difficult to heat a volume of soil evenly to this temperature without specialised equipment. If soil is baked in an oven, for example, some parts of it tend to be heated too much. Small quantities of soil are best pasteurised by being heated in about ½pt of water to around 80° C and then being removed from the source of heat and cooled gradually.

Commercially, soil is now often sterilised by a mixture of steam and air to 60–70° C for ten minutes.

SEED AND POTTING COMPOSTS

Loam composts of the John Innes type supply enough nutrients to last the young seedlings until the pricking-out stage. But loamless sand and peat composts contain very little nutrient and are designed to be used in conjunction with liquid feeding.

Loam composts are easier to manage than loamless ones. During germination, any considerable concentration of fertiliser salts is lethal to the emerging seedlings. Moreover, loamless composts have less buffering capacity than loam composts, so that supplementing fertiliser dressings need to be given in smaller amounts. Nitrogen and chloride of potash are especially damaging to young seedlings, superphosphate much less so. For this reason the John Innes base fertilisers consist of organic, slowly released nitrogen (hoof and horn) together with superphosphate and the sulphate form of potash.

In the formula for loamless seed compost which follows, great care must be taken not to exceed the small quantity of potassium nitrate.

Formulae   *Seed Composts*
              (1cu yd = 21·7 bushels. 1 bushel = 8gal)
John Innes seed compost   *Loamless compost*

3 loam   1 fine sand
1 coarse sand } by volume   1 peat   } by volume
1 peat

	Per bushel	Per cu yd		Per bushel	Per cu yd
Superphosphate	1½oz	2lb	Potassium nitrate	½oz	10oz
Chalk or ground			Superphosphate	1oz	1lb 6oz
limestone	¾oz	1lb	Chalk or		
			limestone	4oz	5¼lb

The John Innes compost contains a relatively large amount of superphosphate, because superphosphate counteracts the toxic effects of the manganese liberated during steam sterilisation of the loam.

The loamless composts need a good deal of chalk or limestone to neutralise the acidity of the sand-peat mixture. But the pH of loamless composts should not exceed pH5, otherwise the trace elements may become unavailable.

PRICKING-OUT COMPOSTS

Formulae   *Pricking-out composts*
                    (1cu yd = 21·7 bushels. 1 bushel = 8gal)

John Innes P1 compost   *Loamless compost*
7 parts sterilized loam   3 parts peat
3 parts peat   1 part sand
2 parts coarse sand

	Per bushel	Per cu yd		Per bushel	Per cu yd
Hoof and horn	1½oz	2lb	Hoof and horn	2oz	2½lb
Superphosphate	1½oz	2lb	Potassium nitrate	½oz	4oz
Sulphate of potash	¾oz	1lb	Superphosphate	1½oz	2lb
Chalk or limestone	¾oz	1lb	Sulphate of potash	⅓oz	4oz
			Chalk or limestone	3oz	4lb
			Magnesian limestone	3½oz	5lb

In the loamless compost, the addition of magnesium is essential. The John Innes P1 compost is also used for sowing tomato and cucumber seeds, which can use a higher level of nutrients at this stage than most other seedlings.

POTTING COMPOSTS

The John Innes P1 pricking-out composts can be converted to potting composts by simply adding two and three times the amounts of fertiliser and lime to the basic mixture. Thus John Innes P2 potting compost is made up as follows:

John Innes P2 potting compost (J.I.P2)   *P3 potting compost (J.I.P3)*
7 parts sterilised loam   7 parts sterilised loam
3 parts peat   3 parts peat
2 parts coarse sand   2 parts coarse sand

J.I.P2

	Per bushel	Per cu yd
Hoof and horn	3oz	4lb
Superphosphate	3oz	4lb
Sulphate of potash	1½oz	2lb
Chalk or limestone	1½oz	2lb

J.I.P3

	Per bushel	Per cu yd
Hoof and horn	4½oz	6lb
Superphosphate	4½oz	6lb
Sulphate of potash	2¼oz	3lb
Chalk or limestone	2¼oz	3lb

The J.I.P2 compost is recommended for plants in the smaller pots, and for lettuces and bedding plants in boxes; the J.I.P3 for tomatoes and chrysanthemums in large pots. These composts contain enough fertilisers for adequate growth without recourse to liquid or supplementary feeding.

The high nutrient levels used in these loam composts cannot be used in loamless composts. But the following peat and sand potting compost has a reasonably lasting supply of plant food:

Loamless potting compost
3 parts peat ⎫
1 part fine sand ⎬ by volume

	Per bushel	Per cu yd
Ammonium nitrate	½oz	10oz
Potassium nitrate	1oz	1lb 5oz
Superphosphate	2oz	2lb 8oz
Magnesian limestone	3oz	4lb
Chalk	3oz	4lb
Trace elements (fritted)	½oz	10oz

While this compost should sustain plants for the greater part of the growing season, those kept in small pots may soon exhaust the available food supply.

Trace elements added to the soil are often fixed in the soil in unavailable forms. This fixation can be avoided by applying them in fritted or chelated form. In the fritted form, the trace elements are fixed into glass-like material. In the chelated form, they are combined with organic materials. Both fritted and chelated trace elements are now commercially available.

Supplementary liquid feeds are usually confined to nitrogen and potassium in approximately equal parts, rather more nitrogen than potassium in the summer. A gallon of concentrate can be made as follows:

> 1lb urea or 1¼lb ammonium nitrate
> 1½lb potassium nitrate
> 1gal water

The concentrate is diluted to 1 in 200 (1tbsp to 5pt of water) and watered on to the plants every ten to fourteen days. The concentrate should be stored in plastic or glass, not metal, containers.

FERTILISATION OF PLANTS GROWN IN CONTAINERS

Plants grown in containers may be fertilised by adding a slowly available dry fertiliser to the soil in the container and, in addition, feeding a dilute liquid fertiliser during the season of growth. Nitrogen, phosphorus and potash may be supplied in dry form in the following mixture:

> 4 parts by weight hoof and horn
> 4 parts by weight superphosphate
> 1 part by weight sulphate of potash

One level tablespoon of the mixture is given to each gallon container, mixed thoroughly with the soil. In addition proprietary liquid fertilisers of grade around 6–6–6 are given at intervals of seven to ten days when the plants are making rapid growth.

ACID COMPOSTS FOR CALCIFUGES

The regular composts are not suitable for azaleas, camellias, heathers or gardenias, but these plants do well in the loamless composts of sand and peat, provided all lime is omitted. The John Innes type of compost, containing loam which has been treated with lime, can be made sufficiently acid by the addition of ¾oz of powdered sulphur in lieu of the ¾oz of chalk or limestone.

M

MIXING AND STORING COMPOSTS

For mixing, the bulk materials – loam, peat and sand – should be spread out on a concrete surface, the loam first, then the moistened peat and then the sand; or in the loamless composts, the peat and then the sand. The materials should be spread out evenly and not heaped up. The sand should be dry. The materials are then thoroughly mixed by shovel.

The lime and fertilisers are added to a quantity of dry sand which runs easily, and are thoroughly mixed. The mixture of sand and fertiliser is then distributed evenly over the bulk materials, the pile being turned and scattered to ensure uniform distribution of the fertiliser.

Composts should be used as soon as possible after mixing. Seed and pricking-out composts which contain organic nitrogen in the form of hoof and horn, etc release much soluble nitrogen in storage which will damage young plants. Such composts should be used within a few days of mixing. When ready-made composts are bought, the lime and fertiliser materials are best packed separately, and only mixed with the bulky material shortly before use.

LIQUID FERTILISERS

Pot plants and greenhouse crops, which have to be watered anyway, are best fed by including dilute nutrient solutions in the water supplies. Strong potting composts such as the John Innes P2 and P3 contain enough nutrients to supply the plants' requirements without the need for much supplementary feeding. But loamless composts contain smaller quantities of nutrients. Moreover, they are quickly leached and therefore need to be used in conjunction with soluble liquid fertilisers. Provided the potting compost contains a supply of the other nutrient elements, the main need is for nitrogen and potassium. A feed of nutrient ratio 1:0:1 is considered adequate for many ornamental plants.

A suitable concentrate has been described in the section on loamless potting composts (see pp182–4). Feeding has to be given in small dilute doses at regular intervals of ten to fourteen days in the growing season.

Most of the readily available inorganic fertilisers are soluble in water. Superphosphate contains about half calcium sulphate and other impurities which do not readily dissolve, but the phosphorus fraction, which is the important fraction, is mostly soluble and the insoluble sediment can be ignored. In making up concentrated solutions of liquid fertiliser, it is best to let the mix stand overnight to allow time for the materials to dissolve fully.

Much has been learnt about liquid fertilisers from hydroponics. The anions in the nutrient solution (nitrates, phosphates and sulphates) need to be considered separately from the cations (calcium, potassium and magnesium). There should be a balance within each group and also between the two groups. Of the anions, phosphorus and sulphur should be present in approximately equal amounts, at about one-third of the nitrogen concentration. Of the cations, potassium and calcium should be present in comparable amounts, while magnesium should be available in lesser quantity, about one-quarter of the amount of potassium.

The monovalent ions, notably nitrate and potassium, are absorbed more readily than the polyvalent ions. It is therefore important to balance nitrogen and potassium so that neither will be taken up in excess to the exclusion of the other essential nutrients.

Since the nutrients are typically supplied in compounds which contain two elements, it is most economic to supply the major elements in sets of twos, as nitrogen and potassium, phosphorus and calcium, magnesium and sulphur. These sets of two could be supplied by potassium nitrate, calcium phosphate and magnesium sulphate. This arrangement has the added advantage that elements of opposite sign (eg potassium and nitrate) are paired in each compound and that all the elements included are used, leaving little or no superfluous residue in the soil. Many other combinations of salts are of course possible. But it is claimed that, at least in water cultures, potassium nitrate is the best form of potassium to use. If potassium chloride is used, for example, the uptake of nitrogen may be depressed.

In practice, some of the more readily available compounds are potassium nitrate (KNO_3) as a source of potassium and nitrogen, treble superphosphate ($Ca(H_2PO_4)_2$) as a source of calcium and phosphorus, and Epsom salts ($MgSO_4 7H_2O$) or kieserite ($MgSO_4 H_2O$) as a source of magnesium and sulphur.

Where the water contains little calcium, calcium nitrate $Ca(NO_3)_2 HO_2$ may be used as a source of calcium and nitrogen. In districts where the water contains much calcium, ammonium dihydrogen phosphate may be used as a source of nitrogen and phosphorus. The amount of nutrient applied at each application will depend on the dilution rate and on the quantity of liquid given. The usual concentration of liquid fertilisers is around 1 in 1,000 or 1,000 parts of solute per million. Then the resulting levels will be reasonably effective whether dry or wet weather follows the application. Stronger solutions are seldom advisable, and may do more harm than good. It is important to realise that about one teaspoon of mixed fertiliser per gallon is all that is required.

The basic requirements are best expressed in parts per million of each element in solution. One hundred parts per million of an element in the fertiliser is equivalent to about 75ppm of the element in the resulting soil solution. The liquid fertiliser therefore has to be rather more concentrated than the soil solution value which it is designed to produce. For the major nutrients the basic requirements are:

	Liquid fertiliser ppm	Resulting soil solution ppm
Nitrogen	200–70	150–200
Phosphorus	60–80	50–60
Potassium	270–400	200–30
Calcium	c270	c200
Magnesium	65	50
Sulphur	80–100	60–80
Total	945–1,185ppm	

In temperate climates and in dull weather the ratio of nitrogen to potash should be about 2:3. In the tropics and in bright sunny weather relatively more nitrogen can be used, giving nitrogen and potassium in equal amounts. For flowers, 150ppm of soil nitrogen is adequate. Only strongly growing vegetables need more.

Liquid fertiliser formulae are conveniently expressed in the amounts of dry materials needed to make up 100l of liquid fertiliser. A typical formula is:

	g/100l	Approximate ppm of fertiliser in solution	
Potassium nitrate	70	92 nitrogen	260 potassium
Calcium nitrate	70	108 nitrogen	144 calcium
Triple superphosphate (monocalcium phosphate)	30	63 phosphorus	42 calcium
Magnesium sulphate	50	48 magnesium	65 sulphur
Total	220g		

This formula provides, in total, 200ppm nitrogen, 63 phosphorus, 260 potassium, 144 calcium, 48 magnesium and 65 sulphur. To each litre of water 2·2g of the mixture would be added. (This is equivalent to approximately 10g or ½oz per gal.)

If plants are growing in loam composts, they may not need a supply of trace elements. But if they are growing in soilless composts, trace elements should be added to the solution or sprayed on to the plants, as described in the section on foliar feeding (see pp190–3).

The concentration of trace elements in the nutrient solution should be of the order:

	ppm
Iron	4·0
Manganese	0·5
Boron	0·5
Zinc	0·1
Copper	0·05
Molybdenum	0·02

The quantities required are so small that it is best to weigh out

1,000 times the amount of each salt required, and then to use the concentrated solution diluted to 1:1,000. Even so, the amounts required to make up a litre of concentrate are small:

Trace-element concentrate		Element at 1,000× required strength ppm
Iron. Ferrous sulphate (20% iron)	20g	4,000
Manganese. Manganese sulphate (25% manganese)	2g	500
Boron. Borax (11% boron)	5·5g	500
Zinc. Zinc sulphate (23% zinc)	440mg	100
Copper. Copper sulphate (25% copper)	200mg	50
Molybdenum. Sodium molybdate (40% molybdenum)	50mg	20

The concentrate should be used at the rate of 1ml/l (or 2tsp per gal) of liquid fertiliser. (Most teaspoons hold about 3ml.)

FOLIAR FEEDING

Plants can absorb liquid nutrients through the leaf as well as from the root, so that foliar (leaf) feeding is possible. The mineral nutrients in foliar sprays are quickly absorbed, but not all nutrients are readily exported from the leaf to other parts of the plant or to other leaves. Calcium and boron, iron and manganese are not readily translocated from the site of their absorption. Most other nutrients, including nitrogen, phosphorus and potassium, are highly mobile.

Foliar feeding by spray can be a useful supplement to nutrition through the root, where soil fertiliser is likely to be fixed, as is phosphorus in acid soils or iron in chalk, or when it may be rapidly leached, as is nitrate in heavy rains. Likewise, foliar feeding may be of advantage when the soil temperature is low, when the soil is badly drained or where a grass sward may intercept top-dressings before they can reach the roots. And certain crops such as gooseberries respond well to foliar feeding. On the other hand it is difficult to give large enough quantities of the major nutrients by the foliar route alone; spraying has to be repeated at frequent intervals. But it is well adapted to supplying trace elements in the very small amounts needed, and this is perhaps its most useful function. Magnesium deficiency is also much more rapidly corrected by foliar spraying than by soil application of magnesium. Magnesium deficiency takes several years to rectify through the soil, but it can be set right in one season by four sprayings at fortnightly intervals, beginning at flowering time, of a 2 per cent solution of Epsom salts.

Considering each nutrient element in turn, of nitrogen fertilisers only urea is satisfactory. Urea is able to penetrate the leaf better than other forms of nitrogen. And the other nitrogen fertilisers burn and scorch the leaves, unless they are used in very dilute solution. Commercially, urea is often sprayed on apple trees, the urea being mixed in with the regular spray materials.

Foliar application of phosphorus is successful in promoting early growth, and since uptake of soil phosphorus fertilisers is often less than 10 per cent of the amount applied, foliar application might be used more widely. But it is difficult to ensure enough phosphorus in the later stages of growth by foliar spray alone.

Potassium in foliar application tends to damage the leaf if potassium chloride is used, and since there are no real difficulties in soil application, there will seldom be any point in abandoning the soil route, unless the soil has a tendency to fix applied potassium.

Magnesium is commonly applied by spray and is more quickly effective than in the soil. Calcium is not usually included in foliar sprays because it is readily taken up from the soil. Sulphate sprayed on leaves is readily absorbed and translocated, and it is seldom included in foliar sprays because it is not often needed.

Iron has often been sprayed on plants which suffer from chlorosis in chalk soils. However, the treatment has not always been successful. Sprayings with ferrous sulphate scorch the leaves badly and the iron, although readily absorbed, is not translocated from the leaf. Foliar feeds now usually include chelated iron.

The other trace elements, boron, manganese, zinc, copper and molybdenum can all be applied in sprays, but boron and copper are more easily applied to the soil. Both copper and zinc need to be mixed with equal amounts of calcium hydroxide (slaked lime), unless very dilute solutions are used, otherwise the leaves are injured.

All foliar sprayings are best carried out just before dark or in the early morning. Absorption is from three to ten times greater in the night than in the day, and greater in the early morning than in the afternoon. High humidity also favours absorption. If the leaves have a waxy surface, so that water runs off them, a proprietary 'wetter' can be used or a little detergent added to the spray.

In summary it can be said that it is pointless to attempt the complete nutrition of the plant by the foliar route, and leaf feeding should therefore be regarded more as a means of supplementing the regular soil nutrition, and of rectifying deficiencies quickly. But it is useful for supplying those nutrients which are omitted from NPK fertilisers and which may be difficult to supply via the soil, notably magnesium, iron and manganese, and other trace elements.

FORMULAE FOR FOLIAR FEEDING

Since it is difficult to supply enough of the major nutrients to have any lasting effect, leaf feeds are usually as highly concentrated as they can be without damaging the leaf. Crystalline urea, which is the preferred source of nitrogen, can be given at the rate of 1oz per gal without damaging most plants, but more than this is likely to scorch the foliage.

Fertiliser materials need to be highly soluble if they are to be applied in a fine spray. This is a source of difficulty with most phosphates: superphosphate, for example, leaves a sediment which will clog spray nozzles. For such reasons it is convenient to use proprietary foliar feeds, provided they contain adequate amounts of the nutrients required.

Nutrient amounts should be higher than those used in soil liquid feeding, and of the following order:

	ppm
Nitrogen (as urea)	500–600
Phosphorus	300–400
Potassium	500–600
Magnesium	500–600
Iron (as iron chelate) and manganese	300–400
Boron, zinc, copper	50–100
Molybdenum	50

Base dressings, which contain trace elements and which are designed for soilless composts, are now commercially available. Foliar and liquid fertilisers, which contain stated amounts of both major and trace elements, are also available.

CHAPTER 10

FERTILISATION OF VEGETABLES, FRUIT AND FLOWERS

> Natural historians tell us that no fruit grows originally
> among us besides hips and haws, acorns and pignuts,
> with other delicacies of like nature; that our climate of
> itself, and without the assistance of art, can make no
> further advances towards a plum than to a sloe, and
> carries an apple to no greater perfection than a crab . . .
> (Addison)

At the outset it should be remembered that light, temperature
and moisture, physical structure and drainage are just as important as the nutrient status of a soil; and that manures and fertilisers will not enable plants to grow in climates to which they
are not adapted or in soils of unsuitable physical condition. Indeed
it is much easier to supply nutrients to a well-drained but infertile
sandy loam than to cultivate an ill-drained although potentially
fertile clay. Often structure and drainage should be improved
before starting a programme of fertilisation.

It is also true that the need for the essential nutrients has been
demonstrated largely on the fast-growing cereals and vegetables
of the temperate zones. If an element has been shown to be essential for one kind of higher plant, it is assumed to be essential for
all other such plants. And yet native species growing in poor
and deficient soils often grow reasonably well, do not appear to
benefit from fertilisation and may even fail to thrive if inorganic
fertilisers are given. Clearly, even if the essential elements are

essential for all higher plants, there are large differences in the quantities of the various elements required by different species; for species have adapted to their environments. On the shallow sandy peats of moorlands the dominant heather, devoid of the usual roothairs, gets its nutrients by means of mycorrhizal associa- tion and survives in acid waterlogged soils by taking up very little water. On the copper-deficient soils of Northern Europe, on which many imported plants fail, native grasses and birches have adapted to the low copper status of the soil. Again, the native plants of salt-marshes can tolerate and use salt concentrations which are lethal to most other plants. And soil acidity is one of the most general selective influences on plant growth. Much of the skill of gardening, in fact, lies not only in supplying the essential elements but in adapting the quantities supplied to the peculiar requirements of the various species.

Much can be inferred from a knowledge of a plant's geographi- cal origins, not only about its climatic but also about its nutrient requirements. The native flowers and shrubs of South Africa or Australia, for example, are unlikely to need much phosphate, since there is little of it in their home soil. But, keeping in mind the great variety of plant life and the many exceptions to any general rules, it is still useful to consider nutrient requirements under the general headings: vegetables, fruit and flowers. The requirements of commercially important crops are of course known with greater precision than the requirements of ornamen- tal plants.

VEGETABLES

Most vegetables are fast-growing annuals which have been selected so as to produce high yields and to respond to large applications of water, manures and fertilisers. Many of them are classed as 'gross feeders', which respond to liberal dressings of farmyard manure. Farmyard manure has been shown to pro- duce greater yields than inorganic fertilisers alone for beets, brassicas, potatoes, turnips and swedes, runner beans, onions and leeks, rhubarb and soft fruit – thus justifying its traditional reputation. Its especial virtue is thought to spring from its power of supplying much soluble potash to young seedlings as well as fair quantities of most of the other nutrients in available form. Nearly all vegetables need a great deal of potassium in early growth. And it is not possible to supply the same lavish amounts of soluble potash by the use of organic fertilisers, without damaging the seedlings and possibly also bringing about magnesium deficiency. But well-made farmyard manure is fast disappearing. The straw which used to absorb the potash-rich urine is now to be seen mouldering in heaps in arable country or is wastefully burnt. Dung unaccompanied by urinated bedding straw is not farmyard manure and is likely to be poor in potassium. At least some of the phosphorus in dung or farmyard manure is also readily available, as well as magnesium, calcium and sulphur.

Many vegetables, especially the leafier sorts, need much nitrogen, together with balancing amounts of all the other essentials. In farmyard manure nearly all the nitrogen is in organic form and is released only slowly, as the soil becomes warm and moist. Most nitrogen fertilisers, on the other hand, and especially nitrates, are immediately available and are either taken up in bulk or leached away and lost. For this reason many market gardeners use organic nitrogen, such as hoof and horn, in the belief that it will release nitrogen in more gradual and continuous fashion. Alternatively, small top-dressings of nitrogen need to be given at intervals. Of the three main fertiliser constituents as applied to most vegetables, the rough rule is that amounts of nitrogen should be balanced by about the same amount of potassium (relatively more potassium is needed by root crops) and that phosphorus should be given at about one-third of the amount of nitrogen. The amounts of nitrogen contained in the aerial parts of plants are often taken as a guide to the quantity of fertiliser to be applied. For phosphorus, however, the amount of fertiliser has to be much higher, since less than 10 per cent of applied phosphorus is retrieved by the more shallow-rooting plants. Potassium, calcium and magnesium amounts are retrieved in intermediate quantities.

Analysis shows that common vegetables can be ranked according to the amounts of nutrients they remove – taking into account the yield and the parts usually harvested:

	Nitrogen	Phosphorus	Potassium	Calcium	Magnesium
High	Potatoes	Brassicas	Tomatoes	Carrots	Tomatoes
	Beans	Tomatoes	Carrots	Tomatoes	Beet
	Carrots	Carrots	Potatoes	Brassicas	Potatoes
	Brassicas		Brassicas	Kidney beans	
Average	Peas	Turnips	Lettuce	Potatoes	Turnips
	Turnips	Kidney beans	Beet	Turnips	Carrots
	Kidney beans	Lettuce	Turnips	Onions	
		Potatoes			
Low	Onions	Onions	Onions	Beet	Beans
	Beet	Beet	Kidney beans	Beans	Peas
	Lettuce	Peas	Beans	Lettuce	
		Beans	Peas	Peas	

It is apparent that vegetables from which high yields are obtained, such as potatoes and tomatoes, need large amounts of all the macronutrients. Brassicas also are heavy consumers of all the elements.

Firm and detailed fertiliser prescriptions cannot be given for all soil types. Much depends on the texture and fertility of soils. Higher amounts of all major nutrients will be required on sandy soils than on clay loams. Apart from differences in soil texture and fertility, fertiliser recommendations for vegetables vary considerably from one country to another. In a warm and favourable climate, very high yields may be possible, necessitating massive fertilisation. In commercial practice, the effort is often to extract the maximum profit from the soil by dense plantings, high-yielding varieties and heavy fertilisation. The amateur grower will usually be content with a more modest yield and will be more interested in quality than quantity. There is evidence that the biological value of vegetables is greater under moderate balanced fertilisation than under heavier and possibly unbalanced fertilisation.

A fair indication of requirements can be derived from consideration of the amounts of the major elements removed, taking into account the yield and the portion of the plant harvested, provided losses and soil interactions are also included in one's calculations. For nitrogen and potassium, some 50 per cent of applied fertiliser should be recovered by the plant. For phosphorus the figure is much less, more of the order of 15–20 per cent, or even less in shallow-rooting crops such as french beans. In the case of phosphorus, the amounts removed in crops may have to be multiplied by a factor of 8 to 10 to arrive at the amount of fertiliser phosphorus required. Potatoes, for example, remove only about 20lb per acre of phosphorus but may be given as much as 200lb of fertiliser phosphorus, being shallow-rooted and grown in soils of low pH.

Before discussing specific requirements, it may be said that the modal recommendation for many vegetables is 80lb nitrogen, 60lb phosphoric acid and 120lb potash per acre. For 1sq rod (30sq yd or $\frac{1}{160}$ acre), which in vegetable plots would be an area 10yd × 3yd, this is 8oz nitrogen, 6oz phosphoric acid and 12oz potash. In terms of fertiliser materials this would be 40oz of sulphate of ammonia (20 per cent nitrogen), 33oz of superphosphate (18 per cent phosphoric acid) and 24oz of sulphate of potash (50 per cent potash).

Now, since vegetables respond so well to farmyard manure, and since farmyard manure will improve soil structure and supply some trace elements, a part of the total requirement should if possible be given as farmyard manure. A ton of farmyard manure is usually taken to contain approximately 10lb nitrogen, 5lb phosphoric acid and 10lb potash. So if 1cwt is applied per rod it should supply 8oz nitrogen, 4oz phosphoric acid and 8oz potash, more if it has been carefully stored and rotted. But the nutrients in farmyard manure are not all available. Only about one-third of the total nitrogen and half the total phosphorus are readily available. Nearly all the potassium is available – but more often than not a good part may have been lost by leaching. The readily available amounts in 1cwt of farmyard manure, unless the ground is warm and speeds up decomposition, are therefore more likely to be of the order of 3oz nitrogen, 2oz phosphoric acid and 6oz potash, leaving a deficit of 5oz nitrogen, 4oz phosphoric acid and 6oz potash to be made up from fertilisers.

The entire sequence of fertilisation stages in preparing a rod ground for vegetables is most simply summarised in a flow diagram:

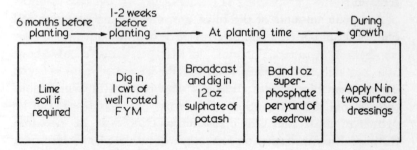

In a garden strip 9ft wide, on average 4 rows of vegetables will be planted. So in 1 rod (3yd × 10yd) of ground, there will be 49 running yards of seed row. In banding fertiliser in a drill to the side of the seed row, the natural tendency is to strew a handful of fertiliser to each yard of the drill. A smallish handful of superphosphate is about 1oz, so that it is fairly easy to spread 1oz per yd evenly along the drill. The total amount given will depend upon the number of rows in the rod of ground. If there are 40yd of row, 40oz of the superphosphate starter would be given. The amount is equivalent to 320lb of superphosphate per acre of 58lb phosphoric acid per acre, which is almost exactly the 60lb phosphoric acid recommended for most vegetables.

Of the other major nutrients, calcium may be required at 10–15oz per rod. Many soils are well enough supplied with this element, and the dressings of lime given to correct acidity, being of the order of ½–1lb per sq yd, will amply ensure the requisite calcium. Magnesium is needed in much smaller amounts, of the order of 1–2oz per rod. In 1cwt of farmyard manure there should be about 10oz of magnesium, but little of it would be in available form. Many limestones, however, contain about 5 per cent of magnesium, so that if ground limestone is used to rectify pH, it could provide enough magnesium for several years. Otherwise, dolomitic limestone could be used instead of ordinary limestone. Removal of sulphur is of the same order as removal of magnesium; the amounts required will normally be amply supplied by rainfall in industrial areas, or by the sulphate contained in other fertilisers.

Adequate amounts of the trace elements manganese, zinc and copper should be supplied by 1cwt of farmyard manure per rod.

BEANS AND PEAS

These vegetables are not especially sensitive to soil reaction, but the soil pH should be above 5·5. Broad beans and peas can be grown in most soils and often succeed in those of moderate fertility. Runner beans, on the other hand, need a deep fertile soil and a regular supply of moisture. Well-rotted farmyard manure is therefore trenched into the subsoil. Dwarf beans need a warm well-drained soil, preferably one that has been manured for a previous crop.

Since the root-nodule bacteria of legumes can fix atmospheric nitrogen, fertiliser, phosphorus and potassium used to be thought more important than nitrogen for legumes generally. But, in fact, symbiotic nitrogen fixation in most beans is much less than in peas. Thus nitrogen needs to be given to runner and dwarf beans (lesser amounts to peas and broad beans). The standard recommendation 8oz nitrogen, 6oz phosphoric acid and 12oz potash therefore serves for runner and dwarf beans, while the amount of nitrogen might be halved for broad beans and peas.

ONIONS AND LEEKS

Neither onions nor leeks will grow well on acid soils. Both need a soil pH of at least 6.

Onions succeeded best on soils which have been manured for a previous crop. A fine tilth and good physical condition are essential. Nitrogen is normally sparingly used in later growth, otherwise maturity may be delayed. On most soils, 6oz nitrogen, 6oz phosphoric acid and 12oz potash should be adequate.

Leeks need a highly fertile soil and generous manuring, including 2–3cwt of farmyard manure per rod. In addition, they should be given the standard 8oz nitrogen, 6oz phosphoric acid and 12oz potash per rod.

SALAD CROPS

Both lettuce and celery are best grown at pH6·5–7·0, lettuce being especially sensitive to the effects of acidity. Cos (romaine) lettuce requires a more fertile soil than the ordinary cabbage lettuce and benefits from a prior dressing of well-rotted farmyard manure. Both lettuce and celery require abundant and continuous moisture.

The standard fertiliser dressing of 8oz nitrogen, 6oz phosphoric acid and 12oz potash is suitable for both crops. But celery demands a much higher level of nutrition than lettuce. It is usually grown commercially in alluvial or fen peat soils and is given the equivalent of some 2–3cwt of farmyard manure per rod.

Spinach is also very sensitive to acidity and needs a pH of 6·5–7·0. It will grow well only on rich and well-drained soil.

BRASSICAS

Brassicas need a pH of 6·0–7·0. Cauliflowers are especially sensitive to acidity, and need a pH of 6·5. Cabbages need a good deal of calcium. In wet climates a preparatory dressing of lime is usually essential.

Abundant moisture is also required. Sandy soils require heavy applications of organic matter and fertiliser.

Cauliflowers need a fertile soil and a great deal of moisture, and are usually given farmyard manure in amounts of 2–3cwt per rod. Other brassicas – brussels sprouts and spring and winter

N

cabbages – do well on ground which has been manured for a previous crop.

The basic fertiliser treatment is 8oz nitrogen, 6oz phosphoric acid and 12oz potash, except for spring greens which are more winter hardy on a diet of less nitrogen and more potash: 4oz nitrogen, 6oz phosphoric acid and 16oz potash.

In addition, all brassicas are given top-dressings of 6–12oz nitrogen in nitrate form once or twice in the growing season, depending on the state of growth of the crop.

POTATOES

Above pH 5·5 potatoes are attacked by an actinomycete which causes scab. Potato soils are therefore not usually limed – although the potato has a quite high calcium requirement. Scab can be controlled by dressing the ground with sulphur. Sulphur not only lowers the pH but is also toxic to the actinomycetes.

Since the yield of potatoes is great (1sq rod should yield over 1cwt of potatoes) correspondingly heavy fertilisation is needed. Farmyard manure is desirable and is best applied well rotted or well in advance of seeding. For a square rod of potatoes 12oz nitrogen, 12oz phosphoric acid and 12oz potash constitutes a suitable dressing. Although the potato is not a heavy consumer of phosphorus, in the acid conditions under which it is usually grown phosphorus is only sparingly available, necessitating high rates of application.

Sprouted seed potatoes are damaged by contact with fertiliser in the soil, and especial care should be taken to band the starter fertiliser so that it does not come into contact with the seed sprouts. Potash should be in the form of sulphate of potash, not chloride of potash, which tends to produce tubers of low dry-matter content.

OTHER ROOT CROPS

Of other root crops, beets, carrots and parsnips grow best in light to medium soils which are free of stones. The optimum pH for beets is 6·5–7·0 and, being halophytic, they benefit from sodium.

Carrots and parsnips are more tolerant of acidity but are best grown around pH6·0. Carrots take up a good deal of calcium. For all these root vegetables the standard fertiliser dressing of 8oz nitrogen, 6oz phosphoric acid and 12oz potash is suitable. But beets are highly responsive to farmyard manure, which should be given well rotted, or some time before seeding.

Swedes and turnips will grow satisfactorily in rather more acid soils than beet, carrots and parsnips, but the pH should be between 5·5 and 6·5. Both these root vegetables need continuous moisture and therefore a good supply of organic matter in the soil. The standard fertiliser dressing is suitable for turnips but swedes are usually given less nitrogen, because high nitrogen is thought to impair keeping quality. On most soils, 4oz nitrogen, 6oz phosphoric acid and 12oz potash per rod would be an appropriate dressing.

Beets, swedes and turnips all have a high boron requirement, and are tolerant of fairly high levels of boron in the soil. On sandy soils especially, they may be given borax (11·3 per cent boron) broadcast at 10–20lb per acre or 1–2oz per sq rod.

TREE FRUIT (APPLES, PEARS, PLUMS)

Tree fruit is grown commercially only in deep loamy soils. The minimum desirable depth of soil is about 2ft and the deeper layers of soil must not be impervious or poorly drained. In texture, very sandy and gravelly soils are generally unsuitable, as are heavy clays at the other extreme. A good deal can be done, however, to adapt trees to local conditions. Apples grown on some dwarfing root-stocks may succeed on shallow soils. Dessert apples are best grown on the lighter well-drained soils. Cooking apples, pears and plums are more adaptable to the heavier soils, need more moisture and will better withstand a wet soil. Cherries, on the other hand, grow well only on very deep well-drained soils.

Since fruit-trees will occupy the ground for many years, and root to a depth of 3ft or more, any nutrient deficiencies should be set right before planting. Most fruit-trees need large supplies of potash and magnesium. An apple tree in full bearing may yield as much as 4cwt of fruit annually which will contain about ½lb potash, besides the amounts needed for tree growth and for the leaves. Although most clay soils have large reserves of potash, the lighter soils do not, and they will not provide adequate supplies. The lighter soils tend to be deficient also in magnesium and since heavy potash dressings which inhibit magnesium uptake are most likely to be given on these soils, it will usually be desirable to increase the stock of magnesium as well. The magnesium requirement is much less than the potash requirement, being more of the order of 1oz per large tree annually.

In dry climates, potash moves down very little in the soil so that, especially under sod, applied potash may not reach the roots. In countries such as South Africa, therefore, potash fertilisers are often placed in furrows which are dug 1ft deep, or in holes dug some 2ft deep in the root zone.

Most fruit-trees grow well in the pH range 5·5–6·5. Lime is required only when the pH is below 5·5. The soil should be limed only to pH6·0, with care taken, especially on the lighter soils, not to raise the pH above this figure. At the same time, apple trees especially need a good deal of calcium, and heavy nitrogen and potassium fertilising in the absence of adequate calcium can lead to bitter pit in the fruit and to other disorders. If it is desired to supply calcium without affecting the soil reaction, it may be given as gypsum or in superphosphate.

Young fruit-trees are usually grown under clean cultivation for four or five years and then grassed down as they come into bearing. The young trees do not then have to compete with grasses for nitrogen and other nutrients. A mulch of farmyard manure or compost is often worked into the soil around the young trees in order to retain moisture and to supply nutrients. For the first few years fertilisers may be broadcast in the root area, which extends somewhat beyond the area covered by branches. During these years little nitrogen fertiliser is required, but as the tree comes into bearing and a grass sward is allowed to grow up around the trees, more nitrogen is required. When orchards are grassed down, the trees get a good supply of nitrogen early but a restricted supply later in the season, as the grasses compete with the trees for the available nitrogen. This is a desirable arrangement since high nitrogen leads to excessive vegetative growth and produces fruit which is over-large, ripens slowly and does not store well, being woody, sweet and otherwise flavourless. When balanced by adequate phosphorus and potassium, fruit matures earlier and is of better keeping quality and more acid flavour.

The rate of nitrogen application will depend on the age and size of the trees, on their planting distances and fruit yields, as well as on the natural fertility of the soil. A rule of thumb is to give 1oz of nitrogen to the young growing tree, increasing this amount in each year by 1oz, so that by the fourth year the tree is getting 4oz nitrogen, equivalent to 40–60lb of nitrogen per acre, depending on planting distances and on the variety. Cooking apples need more nitrogen than dessert apples. As the grass sward grows, the annual amount may be increased to 8oz per tree. The nitrogen is best applied in split dressings: the first in late winter or early spring before grass has started to grow (since fruit-trees are deep-rooted, leaching losses are small); the second in early summer when the flower-buds develop. This second dressing may well be intercepted by the grass cover which therefore should be kept short by frequent mowing or by grazing.

The nitrogen fertiliser needs to be balanced by appropriate amounts of other fertilisers in the ratios 100 nitrogen : 50 phosphorus : 150 potassium; and, if necessary, 100 calcium : 20 magnesium : 20 sulphur. Thus 4oz of nitrogen per tree (eg approximately 1¼lb of nitrochalk) would need to be balanced by 2oz of phosphoric acid (eg about 12oz of superphosphate) and 6oz of potash (eg 12oz of sulphate of potash). The phosphorus and potassium, since they move so slowly in most soils, are best applied in winter so that they will be washed into the soil by rain. Lime or magnesian limestone should also be applied in winter or early spring so as to be washed into the soil before growth begins.

Once the trees are established and a stock of nutrients built up in the soil, the annual potassium dressing should not exceed about 8oz of potash per tree, together with around 4oz of phosphorus and 4oz of magnesium, given every two to three years.

Pears and plums have broadly similar requirements but are said to need more nitrogen and more moisture than apples, while they are less subject to deficiencies of potash and magnesium.

Fruit-trees are thought to need relatively little phosphate, but in soils which are known to be deficient in phosphates – as many clays are – phosphate fertilisers should be applied at the outset. For although the effects of phosphatic fertilisers may not be immediately obvious, experiments in many countries have shown that both yield and quality of fruit are improved by phosphatic manuring. Moreover, many experiments have shown what indeed should have been obvious even since the time of Liebig, that incomplete fertilising with one or two of the macronutrients only, typically nitrogen or potassium, almost inevitably leads to deficiencies of the missing elements.

OTHER TREES AND SHRUBS

In well-drained friable soils, most trees and shrubs once established grow well without the addition of fertilisers, although if they are grassed down and their fallen leaves removed and burnt, old garden trees often show signs of nitrogen and other deficiencies.

In tree-planting, the traditional advice has been to incorporate bulky organic manure into the soil, as leaf-mould, compost, farmyard manure and hop waste, and to follow this treatment with annual mulches of leaf-mould and farmyard manure until the trees or shrubs are well established. Rhododendrons and other shrubs which produce a profusion of blossom certainly benefit from such annual dressings.

Inorganic fertilisers need to be applied with great caution. They are very likely both to damage roots and to scorch foliage, and to prevent seedlings from germinating. This is particularly true of ammonium salts and of the chlorides. Neither the highly soluble inorganic nitrogen fertilisers nor chloride of potash should therefore be applied to the soil at planting or transplanting.

Nevertheless, these substances are now used in commercial tree nurseries in place of the traditional bulky organics, since they are much cheaper per unit of applied nutrients. And in the long term over periods of ten years or more, a combination of organic and inorganic fertilisers gives better results than either alone. Particularly on the lighter, more sandy soils, it is desirable to build up a store of organic residues in the soil in order to conserve moisture and nutrients. In the same way as for fruit-trees, initial soil preparation should include the application of phosphorus, potassium and magnesium fertilisers. But in very sandy soils even potassium fertilisers may be rapidly leached below the root zone and may be better applied as an annual top-dressing. In forest nurseries on sandy soils both nitrogen and potassium may be top-dressed.

The nutrients removed by young trees and shrubs thickly planted in nurseries are estimated to be, in pounds per acre, of the order of: 60 nitrogen, 15 phosphorus, 60 potassium, 40 calcium, 10 magnesium. Assuming that of applied fertilisers only 50 per cent nitrogen, 10 per cent phosphorus, 50 per cent potassium and 50 per cent magnesium are actually absorbed by plants, these amounts become 120 nitrogen, 150 phosphorus, 120 potassium and 20 magnesium and, per sq rod of ground, 12oz nitrogen, 15oz phosphorus, 12oz potassium and 2oz magnesium.

FLOWERS

The exact manurial requirements of the thousands of garden flowers which originate from all over the world are of course unknown, although a good deal is known about flowers of commercial importance such as the rose, carnation and chrysanthemum. But most commonly grown flowers respond to liberal manuring and need a good supply of humus. Hence the preparation of flower-beds, especially for perennials, needs to be exceptionally thorough. The standard advice is to double-dig the ground in the autumn, incorporating manure, compost or peat in the soil.

Flowers which demand a high level of nutrition include roses, chrysanthemums, dahlias, asters and delphiniums, and indeed nearly all those varieties which produce a profusion of blooms over a long period.

Many flowers have a longer growing season than vegetables, most of which grow quickly and are harvested young. And, as the object is to produce flowers rather than leaves, flowers are given less nitrogen than vegetables. Better flowers are produced when nitrogen is restricted, especially after the first growth of the plant. The preference is for slow-acting, balanced manures and fertilisers, which will release nutrients slowly but continuously. Farmyard manure is therefore the first choice, since its nitrogen, being in organic form, is only slowly released. Hoof- and horn-meal, coarsely ground ($\frac{1}{8}$in to dust), is also much used as a slowly available source of nitrogen, together with fish-meal, hop manure and other organic materials. And in general, inorganic nitrogen is used sparingly so as not to encourage an excess of leafy growth.

There are many flowers which will do well on poor soils without fertilisers. Among the annuals are alyssum, Californian poppy, calliopsis, eschscholtzia, godetia, nigella, portulaca, snapdragon and nasturtium. The nasturtium in fact flowers better on a poor soil than on a fertile one. Among shrubs, acacia, broom, cistus, gorse, heather, rhus cotinus and rosemary grow well on poor sandy soils and do not appear to need fertilisers or manures.

ANNUALS

Annuals will grow reasonably well in most soils, provided the soil is about 1ft deep and is not waterlogged. They respond to liberal fertilising and manuring. Beds for annuals and for bedding plants should therefore be dressed with about 1cwt of farmyard manure, compost or peat at the end of the year. If good farmyard manure or compost is available, fertiliser should not be required. If peat, which contains little in the way of nutrients, is used, it should be supplemented by 2lb of superphosphate, mixed with 1lb of hoof and horn per sq rod. On sandy soils and loams 1lb of sulphate of potash should also be added. The fertiliser should be dug well into the soil some weeks before seeding or planting, so as to avoid any possible injury.

Since nearly all annual flowers grow well in a neutral or only slightly acid soil – whereas many fail to thrive in acid soils – the pH should be raised to between 6 and 6·5 by liming with either ground limestone or dolomitic limestone.

PERENNIALS

Deep and thorough preparation of perennial borders is essential. The effort should be to build up organic matter and to place phosphates and potash deep in the root zone. Heavy subsoils should be broken up and the plot should be tile drained, if drainage is poor. The texture of clay soils may be improved by digging in coarse sand, weathered ashes or fine cinders. An amount of 2–3cwt of farmyard manure, compost or peat per sq rod should be well dug in and mixed with the soil.

Since it is difficult to place phosphorus deep enough in the soil once the border has been planted, bone-meal as a slow but lasting source of phosphorus may be dug into the soil in large amounts, up to 7lb per sq rod. If farmyard manure is not available, the bone-meal should be accompanied by 1lb of sulphate of potash or chloride of potash, applied well in advance. Nitrogen is given most economically in liquid form or as a foliar feed in the course of growth. In preparing a bed for perennials the sequence should therefore be:

At end of year	*Early spring*	*A few weeks before planting*
Drain the bed if necessary. Lime if necessary to suitable pH	Double dig and incorporate well-rotted farmyard manure, compost, peat, leafmould or other organic matter	Dig in phosphate and potash

o

ROSES

Most roses grow best on clay loams. Heavier clays suit hybrid perpetuals and rugosa roses, provided drainage is adequate. But good roses can be grown on almost all soils which can be enriched, aerated and drained. If necessary, the rose-bed should be drained by laying a tile drain leading to an outlet.

Roses prefer a slightly acid soil around pH6. If the pH is below 5·5, ground limestone should be dug into the soil as required, but all forms of lime should be applied sparingly.

Good aeration can be ensured by incorporating farmyard manure, compost or peat into the top 24in of soil. In addition, if the soil is a heavy clay, coarse sand or cinders may be mixed with the soil.

The nitrogen requirements of commercial roses are known; and starting from the nitrogen requirement, the amounts of the other essential nutrients can be inferred. Roses are more heavily fertilised than most other flowers, the number of blooms increasing with applied nitrogen up to about 100ppm of nitrate in the soil. Amounts above 150ppm reduce yield. An amount of 100ppm in the soil is equivalent to 200lb of nitrogen per acre (assuming that an acre of topsoil weighs 2 × 10⁶lb) or 20oz of nitrogen per sq rod. But such a high level of soil nitrogen demands massive and frequent fertilisation. About half this level is more appropriate, ie about 50ppm, which is still about twice the amount recommended for most other flowers. This means an application of about 10oz of nitrogen per rod over the season.

This 10oz of nitrogen might be reduced by 2–3oz for each cwt of farmyard manure applied. If peat is used instead of farmyard manure or compost, it should be accompanied by a little manure in order to hasten bacterial decomposition. Failing this, some 2–1–1 fertiliser should be mixed with the peat.

The 10oz of nitrogen might be given in the form of 4–5lb of hoof and horn or other organic fertiliser per rod, in the hope that this will provide a continuous and adequate supply of nitrogen over the growing season; or in the form of a soluble nitrogen fertiliser applied every two or three weeks over the growing season.

Of the possible inorganic fertilisers, ammonium or calcium nitrates produce the best flowers. Sulphate of ammonia, for reasons which are not clear, tends to produce flowers of poor quality. Ammonium nitrate may be applied dissolved in water at the rate of ½oz per 2gal; calcium nitrate at the rate of 10z per 2gal.

The other nutrient elements need to be present in balancing amounts. The 10oz of nitrogen per rod should be accompanied by about 6oz of phosphorus, 10oz of potassium, 10oz of calcium and 1–2oz of magnesium and sulphur, together with much smaller amounts of the trace elements. Undoubtedly the simplest and least complicated course is to apply 2 or 3cwt of well-rotted farmyard manure.

Inorganic fertilisers, especially nitrogen fertilisers and chloride of potash, are likely to damage the roots at planting time. Superphosphate and farmyard manure are safer, but even these should not be in direct contact with roots at planting. Bone-meal therefore tends to be the preferred phosphatic fertiliser, as it can be put into the bottom of planting holes without risk of damage to the roots. But it is probable that 7lb of granulated superphosphate per rod, broadcast and dug in deeply, is more immediately effective than the traditional bone-meal, and it will also supply needed calcium to the lighter and more acid soils.

If farmyard manure is not available, the lighter soils need a dressing of potash in the form of 1–1½lb of sulphate of potash per rod, or 15–20lb of wood ashes, which should be broadcast with the phosphatic fertiliser and well dug in a few weeks before planting. In the absence of farmyard manure, such soils also need magnesium, which is often included in ready-mixed rose fertiliser. The magnesium might be given in the form of 2lb of dolomitic limestone or 2lb of Epsom salts per rod, broadcast and dug into the soil. If trace elements need to be supplied, these are most conveniently given in the form of a complete foliar spraying.

OTHER FLOWERS

Most other flowers do not need the lavish fertilisation given to roses. It is generally agreed that soil nitrogen should be between 25 and 40ppm – 50–80lb per acre or 5–8oz of nitrogen per sq rod – depending on the texture and fertility status of the soil.

Attention to the aeration, drainage and water-retention of the soil is of course just as important as for roses.

The total nitrogen, phosphorus and potassium requirement per rod is likely to be of the order 6oz nitrogen, 6oz phosphorus and 6oz potassium, which could be met by 2cwt of rotted farmyard manure supplemented by about 1lb of superphosphate per rod.

Alternatively, if farmyard manure is not available, 2cwt of granulated peat can be used, dug in with 2lb of calcium nitrate or nitrochalk, 2lb of superphosphates and ¾lb of sulphate of potash, together with 2lb of dolomitic limestone or Epsom salts. Magnesium and trace elements are more likely to be needed on sandy soils. Trace elements, if required, are best supplied in foliar sprays.

REFERENCES

Chapter 1 (pp13–31)

Bonner, J. and Galston, A. W. *Principles of Plant Physiology* (San Francisco: W. H. Freeman, 1952)

Canham, A. E. *Artificial Light in Horticulture* (Eindhoven: Centrex, 1966)

Fritsch, F. E. and Salisbury, E. T. *Plant Form and Function* (London: Bell, 1945)

Gauch, H. *Inorganic Plant Nutrition* (Strondsberg, Pa: Davden, Hutchinson & Ross, 1972)

James, W. O. *Plant Physiology* (London: Oxford University Press, 1963)

Meyer, B. S. and Anderson, D. B. *Plant Physiology* (New York: Van Nostrand, 1952)

Russell, E. W. *Soil Conditions and Plant Growth* (London: Longman, 1961)

Skene, M. *The Biology of Flowering Plants* (London: Sidgwick & Jackson, 1947)

Weaver, J. E. and Clements, F. C. *Plant Ecology* (New York: McGraw-Hill, 1938)

Chapter 2 (pp32–48)

Ahn, P. M. *West African Soils* (London: Oxford University Press, 1970)

Bear, F. E. *Soils in Relation to Crop Growth* (New York: Reinhold, 1965)

Black, C. A. *Soil-Plant Relationships* (New York: Wiley, 1968)

Buckman, H. O. and Brady, N. C. *The Nature and Properties of Soils* (New York: Macmillan, 1960)

Duchaufour, P. *Précis de Pédologie* (Paris: Masson, 1970)

Hall, Sir A. D. *The Soil* (London: Murray, 1921)

Jacks, G. V. *Soil* (London: Nelson, 1954)

Leeper, G. W. *Introduction to Soil Science* (Melbourne: Melbourne University Press, 1964)

Russell, Sir E. J. *The World of the Soil* (London: Collins, 1957)

Thompson, L. M. *Soils and Soil Fertility* (New York: McGraw-Hill, 1957)

Chapter 3   (pp49–71)

Aldous, J. R. *Nursery Practice*, Forestry Commission Bulletin 43 (London: HMSO, 1972)

Bonner, J. and Galston, A. W. *Principles of Plant Physiology* (San Francisco: W. H. Freeman, 1952)

Kohnke, H. *Soil Physics* (New York: McGraw-Hill, 1968)

Malherbe, I. de V. *Soil Fertility* (London: Oxford University Press, 1964)

Russell, E. W. *Soil Conditions and Plant Growth* (London: Longman, 1961)

Thompson, L. M. *Soils and Soil Fertility* (New York: McGraw-Hill, 1957)

Winter, E. J. 'Watering for Amateurs', *Jnl Royal Horticultural Society*, vol 97 (August 1972), 361–8

Chapters 4 and 5   (pp72–122)

Bear, F. E. *Soils in Relation to Crop Growth* (New York: Reinhold, 1965)

Berger, K. C. *Introductory Soils* (London: Collier-Macmillan, 1965)

Black, C. A. *Soil-Plant Relationships* (New York: Wiley, 1968)

Cooke, G. W. *The Control of Soil Fertility* (London: Crosby Lockwood, 1966)

——. *Fertilizing for Maximum Yield* (London: Crosby Lockwood, 1972)

Dermott, W. and Eagle, D. J. (eds). *Soil Potassium and Magnesium*, Ministry of Agriculture Technical Bulletin 14 (London: HMSO, 1967)

Dinauer, R. C. (ed). *Changing Patterns in Fertiliser Use* (Madison, Wisconsin: Soil Science Society of America, 1968)

Fried, M. and Broeshart, H. *The Soil-Plant System* (London: Academic Press, 1967)

Gericke, W. F. *Soilless Gardening* (London: Putnam, 1940)

Hopkins, D. P. *Chemicals, Humus and the Soil* (London: Faber & Faber, 1945)

Ignatieff, V. and Page, H. J. (eds). *Efficient Use of Fertilisers* (Rome: FAO, 1958)

Leeper, G. W. *Introduction to Soil Science* (Melbourne: Melbourne University Press, 1964)

Malherbe, I. de V. *Soil Fertility* (Cape Town: Oxford University Press, 1964)

Meyer, B. S. and Anderson, D. B. *Plant Physiology* (New York: Van Nostrand, 1952)

Page, E. R. 'Fertilisers may increase yields but they can also decrease emergence', *The Grower*, vol 80, no 9 (1973), 393–5

Paisley, K. *Fertilisers and Manures* (London: Collingridge, 1960)

Russell, E. J. *Soils and Manures* (London: Cambridge University Press, 1919)

Russell, Sir E. J. *The World of the Soil* (London: Collins, 1957)

Smith, A. M. *Manures and Fertilisers* (London: Nelson, 1952)

Thompson, L. M. *Soils and Soil Fertility* (New York: McGraw-Hill, 1957)

Tisdale, S. L. and Nelson, W. L. *Soil Fertility and Fertilisers* (London: Collier-Macmillan, 1966)

Vanstone, E. *Fertilisers and Manures* (London: Macmillan, 1947)

Voisin, A. *Fertiliser Application* (London: Crosby Lockwood, 1965)

Chapter 6 (pp123–38)

Comber, N. M. *et al. An Introduction to Agricultural Chemistry* (London: Edward Arnold, 1964)

Cooke, G. W. *The Control of Soil Fertility* (London: Crosby Lockwood, 1966)

Hooper, L. J. and Eagle, D. J. (eds). *Nitrogen and Soil Organic Matter*, Ministry of Agriculture Technical Bulletin 15 (London: HMSO, 1969)

Hopkins, D. P. *Chemicals, Humus and the Soil* (London: Faber & Faber, 1945)

Jacks, G. V. *Soil* (London: Nelson, 1954)

Paisley, K. *Fertilisers and Manures* (London: Collingridge, 1960)

Robinson, G. W. *Mother Earth* (London: Murby, 1947)

Russell, E. J. *Soils and Manures* (London: Cambridge University Press, 1919)

Russell, Sir E. J. *Soil Conditions and Plant Growth* (London: Longman, 9th ed 1961)

Simons, A. J. *The Vegetable Grower's Handbook* (London: Penguin, 1948)

Stefferud, A. (ed). *Soil*, US Department of Agriculture Yearbook 1957 (Washington, DC: US Govt Printing Office)

Chapter 7   (pp139–59)

Bear, F. E. *Soils in Relation to Crop Growth* (New York: Reinhold, 1965)

Coleman, N. T. and Mehlich, A. 'The Chemistry of Soil pH', *Soil*, US Department of Agriculture Yearbook 1957 (Washington, DC: US Govt Printing Office)

Cooke, G. W. *The Control of Soil Fertility* (London: Crosby Lockwood, 1967)

Gardner, H. W. and Garner, H. V. *The Use of Lime in British Agriculture* (London: E. & F. Spon, 1957)

Hall, Sir A. D. *The Soil* (London: Murray. New and revised ed Robinson, W. (ed) 1945)

Hanna, W. J. and Hutcheson, T. B. 'Soil–Plant Relationship', chap 6, Nelson, L. B. *Changing Patterns in Fertiliser Use* (Madison, Wisconsin: Soil Science Society of America, 1968)

Leeper, G. W. *Introduction to Soil Science* (Melbourne: Melbourne University Press, 4th ed 1964)

Lloyd, C. *Gardening on Chalk and Lime* (London: Pan Books, 1969)

Osborn, A. *Shrubs and Trees for the Garden* (London: Ward Lock, 1931)

Robinson, W. *The English Flower Garden* (London: Murray. Revised ed Hay, R. (ed) 1956)

Salisbury, Sir E. J. *The Living Garden* (London: Bell, 1949)

Chapter 8   (pp160–77)

Berger, K. C. *Introductory Soils* (London: Collier-Macmillan, 1965)

Bould, C. 'The Mineral Nutrition of Plants I', *Jnl Royal Horticultural Society*, vol 97 (1972), 218–25

Hewitt, E. J. 'The Essential Nutrient Elements', Steward, F. C. (ed), *Plant Physiology*, vol III (London: Academic Press, 1963)

Schutte, K. H. *The Biology of the Trace Elements* (London: Crosby Lockwood, 1964)

Stiles, W. *Trace Elements in Plants* (London: Cambridge University Press, 1961)

Viets, F. G. 'Soil Testing for Micronutrients', *Soil Testing*, special publication series, no 2 (Madison, Wisconsin: Soil Science Society of America, 1967)

Wallace, T. *The Diagnosis of Mineral Deficiencies in Plants by Visual Symptoms* (London: HMSO, 1961)

Webber, J. (ed). *Trace Elements in Soils and Crops*, Ministry of Agriculture, Fisheries and Food Technical Bulletin 21 (London: HMSO, 1971)

Chapter 9 (pp178-93)

Douglas, J. S. *Hydroponics* (London: Oxford University Press, 4th ed 1959)

Gericke, W. F. *Soilless Gardening* (London: Pitman, 1940)

Harris, D. *Hydroponics* (Newton Abbot: David & Charles, 1974)

Hartmann, H. T. and Kester, D. E. *Plant Propagation* (New York: Prentice-Hall, 1959)

Hume, W. G. (ed). *Pot Plants*, Ministry of Agriculture Bulletin 112 (London: HMSO, 1969)

Lawrence, W. J. C. and Newell, J. *Seed and Potting Composts* (London: Allen & Unwin, 1962)

Winsor, G. W. 'Nitrogen and Glasshouse Crops', *Nitrogen and Soil Organic Matter*, Ministry of Agriculture Technical Bulletin 15 (London: HMSO, 1969)

Chapter 10 (pp194-212)

Cooke, G. W. *Fertilizing for Maximum Yield* (London: Crosby Lockwood, 1972)

Christopher, E. P. *Introductory Horticulture* (New York: McGraw-Hill, 1958)

Ede, R. (ed). *Soils and Manures for Vegetables*, Ministry of Agriculture Bulletin 71 (London: HMSO, 1968)

——. *Soils and Manures for Fruit*, Ministry of Agriculture Bulletin 107 (London: HMSO, 1964)

Fried, M. and Broeshart, H. *The Soil-Plant System* (London: Academic Press, 1967)

Gardner, V. R. *et al. Fruit Production* (New York: McGraw-Hill, 1952)

Hartmann, H. T. and Kester, D. E. *Plant Propagation* (New York: Prentice-Hall, 1959)

Hooper, L. J. and Eagle, D. J. (eds). *Nitrogen and Soil Organic Matter*, Ministry of Agriculture Technical Bulletin 15 (London: HMSO, 1969)

Hume, W. G. (ed). *Pot Plants*, Ministry of Agriculture Bulletin 112 (London: HMSO, 1969)

Laurie, A. and Ries, V. *Floriculture* (New York: McGraw-Hill, 1950)

Nelson, L. B. (ed). *Changing Patterns in Fertiliser Use* (Madison, Wisconsin: Soil Science Society of America, 1968)

Osborne, A. *Shrubs and Trees* (London: Ward Lock, 1963)

Paisley, K. *Fertiliser and Manures* (London: Collingridge, 1960)

Sutton & Sons. *The Culture of Vegetables and Flowers* (London: Simpkin Marshall, 1930)

Yates, A. *Garden Guide* (Sydney: Angus & Robertson, 1965)

CONVERSION TABLES

LENGTH

Metric	Imperial
10Å = 1mμ	12in = 1ft
1,000mμ = 1μ (1 micron)	3ft = 1yd
1,000μ = 1mm	1,760yd = 1 mile
10mm = 1cm	
100cm = 1m	
1,000m = 1km	

Metric to Imperial	Imperial to Metric
1mm = 0·03937in	1in = 2·54cm
1cm = 0·3937in	1ft = 0·3048m
1m = 39·37in or 1·094yd	1yd = 0·9144mm

AREA

Metric	Imperial
1 are = 100sq m	1 acre = 4,840sq yd
1 hectare = 10,000sq m	1 sq rod = 30·25sq yd
	160sq rods = 1 acre

Metric to Imperial	Imperial to Metric
1sq m = 1·196sq yd	1sq yd = 0·8361sq m
1 are = 119·6sq yd	1sq rod = 25·29sq m
1 hectare = 2·4711 acres	1 acre = 0·40468ha

CAPACITY

Metric	*Imperial*
1,000ml = 1l	20fl oz = 1pt
	8pt = 1gal
	8gal = 1 bushel

Metric to Imperial	*Imperial to Metric*
1l = $\begin{cases} 35\cdot2\text{fl oz} \\ 1\cdot759\text{imp pt} \\ 0\cdot22\text{imp gal} \end{cases}$	1fl oz = 0·028351
	1imp pt = 0·568l
	1imp gal = 4·546l

WEIGHT

Metric	*Imperial*
1,000mg = 1g	437·5 grains = 1oz
1,000g = 1kg	16oz = 1lb
100kg = 1 quintal	112lb = 1cwt
10 quintals = 1 metric ton	2,240lb = 1 ton

Metric to Imperial	*Imperial to Metric*
1mg = 0·015 grains	1oz = 28·35g
1g = 15·432 grains	1lb = 0·4536kg
10g = 0·353oz	1cwt = 50·8kg
1kg = 2·204lb or 35·27oz	1 ton = 1,016kg
1 quintal = 220·46lb	

OTHER USEFUL CONVERSIONS

SOLUTIONS

oz per gal × 6·25	= g per l
g per l × 0·16	= oz per gal
1 grain per gal	= 14·3ppm
lb/acre × 1·121	= kg/hectare
1 ton per acre	= 0·4628lb per sq yd
1gal water (at 62° F)	= 10lb
1l water (at 4° C)	= 1,000g = 1kg
1 part per million (1ppm)	= 1lb per 100,000gal or 1mg per kg

10lb per acre $=$ 10z per sq rod
1cwt per acre $= \frac{3}{8}$oz per sq yard (approx) (more exactly 0·370oz)
1in of water $=$ 22,622gal per acre
                   $= 4\frac{1}{2}$gal per sq yd
1 atmosphere $=$ 29·92in of mercury
                  $=$ 34ft of water $=$ 14·7lb per sq in

ELEMENTS TO 'OXIDES'	'OXIDES' TO ELEMENTS
$2\frac{1}{3} \times P = P_2O_5$	$P = \frac{3}{7} \times P_2O_5$
$1\frac{1}{5} \times K = K_2O$	$K = \frac{5}{6} \times K_2O$
$1\frac{2}{5} \times Ca = CaO$	$Ca = \frac{5}{7} \times CaO$
$1\frac{2}{3} \times Mg = MgO$	$Mg = \frac{3}{5} \times MgO$

1 British gal $=$ 1·20094 US gal
1 US gal $=$ 0·83268 British gal
1cu ft $=$ 6·25 British gal

INDEX